Modern Peacemakers

Shirin Ebadi

Champion for Human Rights in Iran

MODERN PEACEMAKERS

Modern Peacemakers

Shirin Ebadi

Champion for Human Rights in Iran

Janet Hubbard-Brown

CHELSEA HOUSE
PUBLISHERS

An imprint of Infobase Publishing

Shirin Ebadi

$30.00

Copyright © 2007 by Infobase Publishing

Chelsea House
An imprint of Infobase Publishing
132 West 31st Street
New York NY 10001

ISBN-10: 0-7910-9434-0
ISBN-13: 978-0-7910-9434-1

Library of Congress Cataloging-in-Publication Data
Hubbard-Brown, Janet.
    Shirin Ebadi, champion for human rights in Iran / Janet Hubbard-Brown.
        p. cm. — (Modern peacemakers)
    Includes bibliographical references and index.
    ISBN 0-7910-9434-0 (hardcover)
    1. 'Ibadi, Shirin. 2. Women lawyers—Iran—Biography. 3. Lawyers—Iran—Biography. 4. Women judges—Iran—Biography. 5. Judges—Iran—Biography. 6. Nobel Prize winners—Iran—Biography. 7. Iran—Politics and government—1979-1997. 8. Iran—Politics and government—1997- I. Title. II. Series.
    KMH110.I23H83 2007
    323.092--dc22
    [B]   2006033628

Text design by Annie O'Donnell
Cover design by Takeshi Takahashi

Printed in the United States of America

Bang FOF 10 9 8 7 6 5 4 3 2 1

This book is printed on acid-free paper.

TABLE OF CONTENTS

CHAPTER 1

Reign of Terror

On November 22, 1998, two Iranian intellectuals, husband and wife Dariush and Parvaneh Forouhar, were brutally murdered in their home in Tehran. Soon afterward, a translator named Majid Sharif disappeared. His body was later found at the coroner's office. Ten days later, writer Mohammad Mokhtari went out to buy lightbulbs and also disappeared. Officials at the morgue determined that he had been suffocated. On the day Sharif's body was discovered, another writer, Mohammad Jafar Pouyandeh, disappeared; following the same pattern, his body was found at the coroner's office on December 13.[1]

The list goes on. The serial murders were horrifying even to the Iranian people, who had lived through a major revolution and an eight-year war with Iraq. The murders were also perplexing: Beginning in 1997 with the election of President Seyyed Muhammad Khatami, interference in citizens' private lives had lessened—under the new reformist leader, people were enjoying more freedom. The supreme leader of Iran, Ayatollah Ali Khamenei, claimed to be shocked, and President Khatami called the murders "disgusting acts aimed at bringing down the Islamic system."[2]

1

Iran had become the Islamic Republic of Iran after the shah, or king, was overthrown in 1979, and militant religious leaders replaced the secular government. When the government was reorganized, the elected president and others in the secular division of the government were placed directly under the control of the ayatollah and the clerics, diminishing their power.

Shirin Ebadi was a lawyer who had been stripped of her judgeship after the 1979 Iranian Revolution because she was a woman. She was nervous when she heard about the 1998 murders. After the revolution, Ebadi had refused to accept a menial job as a clerk in the courtroom where she had been a judge. Instead, she eventually decided to do legal work pro bono, helping those who could not afford a lawyer to fight for family members who had been unjustly accused or killed. A petite woman less than five feet tall, Ebadi was approached by Parastou Forouhar, the daughter of the slain intellectuals. Forouhar wanted her help in investigating her parents' deaths. Ebadi agreed to take the case. Like detectives, the two women tried to piece together what had happened. They questioned the police, neighbors, and household servants in their search for clues.

The murdered couple, who had been outspoken critics of the religious regime, had been members of the Iran Nation Party (*Hezb-e Mellat-e Iran*). The group was founded in the 1950s, when Prime Minister Mohammad Mossadeq was the country's first democratically elected leader. Loved by the people, he had been a strong advocate for women's rights, a civil society, and religious freedom. He clashed with the reigning monarch, Reza Shah, over who would control the army, and Mossadeq won. The next battle was over oil. Mossadeq decided to nationalize the oil industry, but the shah, the leading clerics, and the governments of Great Britain and America were opposed. There was too much profit involved. Eventually, Mossadeq was violently overthrown. He was convicted of treason and kept in solitary confinement for three years before being placed under house arrest until his death in 1967 at the age of 85.

When the Forouhars were murdered in 1998, the Iran Nation Party consisted mainly of aging intellectuals and a few college students. "They were no more dangerous to the Islamic regime than a storm of down feathers," Shirin Ebadi wrote in her memoir.[3] Their only crime was being openly critical of the Iranian constitution and the supreme leader, who they thought had too much power—the kinds of complaints that Americans are allowed to voice wherever and whenever they choose. The Ministry of Intelligence and Security (MOIS) harassed the couple constantly, and even went after their children, who eventually moved to Germany because of the harrasment and interrogations.

On the evening of the murders, Mr. Forouhar was entertaining guests. Suddenly, one of the guests jumped up and tied Mr. Forouhar to a chair. They proceeded to stab him 11 times, then turned his lifeless body toward Mecca, the holy city according to Islam. The attackers found his wife upstairs, preparing to go to bed; they stabbed her 24 times. The bodies were discovered the next day. Mrs. Forouhar's poetry and Mr. Forouhar's diary, which included his correspondence with Prime Minister Mossadeq, were later reported missing.

Another shock followed on January 6, 1999. Under growing pressure from the people, for the first time in the history of the Islamic Republic of Iran, the government accepted partial responsibility for the killings of government critics. They laid blame for the crimes on a rogue gang within the Ministry of Intelligence and Security, denying that anyone with seniority had been involved. A 39-year-old investigative journalist named Akbar Ganji, however, penetrated the Iranian intelligence organization, intending to find the secret state plan to eliminate critics of the government. He discovered that senior clerics had issued *fatwas,* or Islamic decrees, that served as death sentences; he boldly wrote articles about his findings, which the Iranian people rushed out to buy. The short-lived freedom of the press was brought to an abrupt halt when the hardline judiciary shut down a popular independent newspaper called *Salaam.* Other

Shirin Ebadi (right) and Parastou Forouhar (left) converse in front of a portrait of Iranian nationalist Dariush Forouhar. When Forouhar and his wife, Parvaneh Eskandari, were murdered under suspicious circumstances, their daughter, Parastou, went to Ebadi for help.

media closures followed. Students protested, and within days, riots broke out. President Khatami, who had worked hard for reform, turned against the students. He felt that the riots, which caused more deaths, were the price he had been forced to pay for holding the state accountable for the murders.

Because of the negative publicity generated by the 1998 assassinations, the government agreed to allow the lawyers representing the victims' families to have access to the files containing accounts of those events. They were given only 10 days to read thousands of pages and were not permitted to make photocopies. There would be a trial, but it would be closed-door, and a gag order was placed on all attorneys. The lawyers, including Shirin Ebadi, met with the intention of reading as much as they possibly could. She was selected to read the pages concurrently, and the rest would read them randomly. To make their task more daunting, officials had buried the testimonies in mountains of bureaucratic papers. By late afternoon, Ebadi, exhausted, had a cup of tea and continued to read. She came to a page that had more narrative than the others. It was a transcript of a conversation between a member of a death squad and a government minister. Ebadi read: "The next person to be killed is Shirin Ebadi."

She read it over and over, then turned to Parastou Forouhar to show her the page. They read that the minister, when asked by the assassin if he could murder Ebadi, had replied that he should wait until after Ramadan, the Islamic month of fasting. The assassin complained that people like Ebadi did not fast—that they had divorced God. He wanted to kill her immediately. Ebadi's life had hung in the balance and she had known nothing about it: If the minister had relented, she would have been killed.

Ebadi and Parastou pressed on. At the end of the day, Ebadi told the other lawyers about how close she had come to being murdered. They shook their heads and expressed gratitude that she had not been killed. She took a taxi home, and in her words, "ran inside, peeled off my clothes and stayed under the shower for an hour, letting the water cascade over me, rinsing off the filth of those files."[4]

Her abstract worry had now turned to real fear. When would she be killed? Where would she be when it happened? She would have to learn to live with fear and to control it, lest it overwhelm her.

The final sentencing of those accused of murdering the Forouhars was disappointing to the defending lawyers—two suspects were sentenced to life imprisonment, the assassins were sentenced to death, and other conspirators received short prison terms. The Iranian Supreme Court overturned some of those verdicts, but no one would ever know which ones. The lawyers were told that the information had to remain a secret in the interest of national security. Even though Ebadi felt that she had not been successful in bringing the killers to justice, something more far-reaching had occurred: The families of other dissidents started coming to Ebadi. A code of silence had been broken.

The repression continued, however. In 2000, Akbar Ganji attended a conference in Berlin, Germany. When he returned, he was accused of being "anti-Islamic" and was sentenced to 10 years in prison. His sentence was eventually appealed, but in the end, he was imprisoned for six years on charges of collecting papers that could harm national security. At his trial, he was represented by three lawyers, one of whom was Shirin Ebadi. In 2003, students at various universities began to call for the end of the Islamic system of government. They were brutally attacked by government forces. Over six days, 4,000 students went missing. During that time, a young Iranian-Canadian photographer was murdered. Her parents went to Shirin Ebadi, who agreed to serve as their lawyer. During that same year, 56-year-old Ebadi was awarded the Nobel Peace Prize. She wrote,

> When I heard the statement of the prize read aloud, heard my religion mentioned specifically alongside my work defending Iranians' rights, I knew at that moment what was being recognized: the belief in a positive interpretation of Islam, and the power of that belief to aid Iranians who aspire to peacefully transform their country.[5]

Iranian dissident and investigative reporter Akbar Ganji holds up his Golden Pen of Freedom award, presented to him by the World Association of Newspapers at their May 2006 meeting in Moscow. Six years earlier, in 2000, Ganji had been sentenced to a prison term by the Iranian govern ment on charges of endangering national security.

Although the Iranian press had been instructed to downplay the prize, when Ebadi arrived at the airport on her way to accept the prize, a crowd stretched out as far as she could see. There were hundreds of thousands of people, spread out in all directions, the majority of them women. Ebadi said, "Some wore the black chador, but most bright veils, and the gladioluses and white roses they waved in the air flashed in the dark of the night."[6] Ebadi's brother told her that they had walked to be there to greet the woman who had worked nonstop for their cause. Ebadi already knew her next task, which would seem insurmountable to most: She would need to use her fame to convince the world that Iran could be changed through reform, without violence.

CHAPTER 2

Girl in Iran

Shirin (a name derived from the Farsi word meaning "sweet") Ebadi was born on June 21, 1947, in Hamedan, Iran, a province in central-western Iran, 180 miles from the capital city of Tehran. Both of her parents had been raised there, and her father, a lawyer, was comfortable in his job as the deputy minister of agriculture. Iran is slightly larger than the state of Alaska. It is situated between Iraq and Pakistan, and borders the Persian Gulf, the Gulf of Oman, and the Caspian Sea. Other land borders include Afghanistan, Armenia, Turkey, Turkmenistan, and Azerbaijan.

When she was a year old, Shirin, her parents, and her older sister moved to a big house in Tehran. For years afterward, they would travel back and forth between the city and Shirin's birthplace. The house in Tehran was built around a central courtyard garden. In her memoirs, Ebadi described one of her happiest visual memories: The courtyard, filled with roses and white lilies, surrounded a pool that contained silvery fish. At night during the summer, the children's beds were moved outside, and they would sleep under the stars. Four

A view of Tehran, the capital city of Iran, appears above in a photograph from 1978. When she was a year old, Shirin Ebadi moved with her family to a big house in Tehran.

servants, who had followed the family from the farm in Hamedan, came to live with them; each was assigned a specific role.

It would have been an idyllic life for the four Ebadi children, except for a shadow that hung over the household: Their mother, Minu, suffered from a mental malaise that caused anxieties that sometimes incapacitated her. She was fearful if her children returned home five minutes late, and she eventually developed physical ailments, including asthma. "I can't recall a single day when my mother seemed truly happy,"[7] Ebadi wrote in her memoir. Even with such an emotional handicap, though, Minu Ebadi made her children her life. She believed that being a good mother was a woman's most important role.

Ebadi's father, Mohammad-Ali Khan, had been born into a family of wealthy landowners. His father had been a colonel in the military in the last days of the Qajar Dynasty, which preceded the monarchy of Ebadi's childhood. He had fallen in love with and married a princess, but when it was learned that she was unable to bear children, he, with her approval, married a second wife—a relatively common practice at the time. His second wife, Shahrbanu, gave birth to two sons, one of whom was

Shirin Ebadi's father. When Mohammad-Ali Khan was seven, his father died, and Shahrbanu had to fight hard to keep her children and the holdings that remained. She went to the clerics in Iran's holiest city, Qom, to implore them to help her, for in those days petitioning the legal system was unheard of.[8]

Ebadi's parents, Minu and Mohammad-Ali, married in 1941 in the traditional way, through a courtship ritual known as *khastegari.* They met at a relative's house, and Ebadi's father presented himself at her family's home a few months later, to ask for her hand in marriage. It was obvious that he was very in love with the beautiful young woman, and she grew to love him deeply. The marriage meant an end to her dream of becoming a doctor, however, which might account for her later depression.

A BRIEF HISTORY

At the beginning of the twentieth century, the goverment of Iran was in a state of flux. Russia and Great Britain wielded great influence in Tehran at that time, though the nation was never colonized, unlike many of its neighbors. But domestic affairs, along with the rise of modernization throughout the world, were brewing change. When the governor of Tehran wanted to punish some sugar merchants for refusing to lower prices in 1905, a group of tradesmen, merchants, and *mullahs* (Shia Muslim religious leaders) hid in a mosque and then in a shrine until the mayor agreed to create a "House of Justice." It was never established, but a violent protest of students and clerics demanding the formation of a *Majlis,* or legislative assembly, came next, and the shah agreed to those terms. The first Majlis (or National Assembly) met in October 1906 and began to write a constitution, which became law that December. The old shah died, and the new king signed a Supplementary Fundamental Law. The two documents became the core of the Iranian Constitution.

Fearful that the National Assembly would have too much power, the shah, colonial leaders, and revolutionaries rebelled.

In response, the Russians demanded certain conditions and were refused. The Russians killed some of the leaders, stormed the Majlis, and dissolved it. The parliament and constitution remained, but their power was greatly weakened.

When World War I began in 1918, Iran's economy was in terrible shape. In 1921, the self-named Reza Khan entered Tehran with soldiers and insisted that the cabinet be dissolved and that he be given control of the military. By 1923, he was appointed prime minister. The shah from the Qajar Dynasty left the country. In 1925, his dynasty, which had ruled Iran since 1785, was deposed. Reza Khan named himself shah and created the Pahlavi Dynasty.

The new shah developed some popular support. He brought about reforms in education and law, which until then had been under the control of the clergy. Hundreds of schools were built after the shah demanded compulsory education. One of his first steps was to empower women, for he believed he needed their participation in the government. As early as 1932, the Oriental Feminine Congress met in Tehran; the group called for women to be given the right to vote, compulsory education for boys and girls, equal salaries for men and women, and an end to polygamy.[9]

The shah banned the veil worn by traditionalist women, whose philosophy was deeply embedded in a conservative interpretation of the Koran—which is to Muslims what the Bible is to Christians. (Ebadi referred to the veil as "the symbol of the tradition's yoke."[10]) For many of the women affected, the new ban was devastating. Because Shirin's mother's family was not traditional, they were mostly unaffected by the new law, though, and more and more women from middle-class and elite families came to perceive the veil as a symbol of oppression. It was the first time a politician had "acted out a political agenda on the frontier of women's bodies," Ebadi remarked.[11]

As Reza Shah's alliance with the United States grew stronger, Russia withdrew from Iran. First, though, Iran fell under Anglo–Soviet occupation. In 1939, the year Shirin Ebadi's parents married, World War II broke out, and British and Russian forces occupied Iran. Reza Shah was forced to abdicate (give up) his throne to his son, Mohammad Reza Pahlavi, in 1941, after the British and the Russians concluded that Reza Shah

The Veil

French writer Guy de Maupassant once described women in chadors as "death out for a walk." Many Westerners perceive veiling as either a prison—a symbol of oppression—or an erotic symbol, associated with harems.

The Islamic tradition of *hijab*, or covering, is supposed to be voluntary and to extend to men as well, who also should not reveal too much of their bodies in public. Originally, upper-class women among the Jews, Persians, and other cultures veiled, and the veils were not black. Rural and nomadic women needed full bodily movement in order to work outdoors, so they often did not veil.

The practice of separating and covering women began with the Greek Christians and was later adopted by the Muslims. Head or body covering usually arises during periods when Muslim countries feel threatened. The Mongol invasions of Iraq and Iran in the sixteenth century caused women to seek protection by covering. Similarly, during colonization of their countries, some Muslim women wore the veil in defiance of Western styles. Today, the significance of veiling depends on local and family customs.

Part of the negative reaction to veiling in modern times in Iran has to do with the fact that women are commanded to veil or unveil by various male rulers. Geraldine Brooks wrote in her book, *Nine Parts of Desire: The Hidden World of Islamic Women,*

In the end, under all the concealing devices—the chador, jalabiya or abaya, roosarie, or shayla—was the body. And under all the talk about hijab freeing women from commercial or sexual exploitation, all the discussion of hijab's potency as a political and revolutionary symbol of selfhood, was the body:

had pro-Nazi tendencies. The British also needed Iran's vast oil resources and access to the Persian Gulf, so they may have wanted an Iranian ruler whom they thought they could manipulate more easily. The new shah was only 22 years old and was

the dangerous female body that somehow, in Muslim society, had been made to carry the heavy burden of male honor.*

In 1935, when the shah banned the wearing of the veil, traditional women tried to fit their waist-length hair under a French cloche. They were terrified of being attacked by soldiers if they went out with the veil, so they would not leave their homes. After the veiling rule was lifted, they were ridiculed if they wore them. Not even a month after Ayatollah Khomeini the 1979 Revolution in Iran, women were ordered to veil themselves in public. Then, it was the unveiled women who were ridiculed, and worse, severely punished if they disobeyed.

Everything had to be covered except the eyes. Most adopted the chador, a tentlike structure made out of two pieces of fabric with no buttons or hooks, which is thrown over the head and falls to the ankles. The woman has to hold it in place by clutching the cloth under the chin. If she has to carry something, she holds the fabric in her teeth. According to one writer, chadors are worn by only about 20 percent of women in Tehran today. The law of covering implemented by Ayatollah Khomeini is still in effect, but women are not being dragged off the streets and lashed if any skin is exposed. Most women prefer the headscarf and ankle-length coat. It is often mentioned in Western periodicals that when touring North America, Shirin Ebadi does not cover her head as an act of rebellion. The truth is that, to most Islamic women, the veil is not a great issue when they are fighting for their right to freedom of speech. With the highest rate of education among women in the world, the women of Iran have not allowed the veil to keep them in a domestic prison.

*Geraldine Brooks, *Nine Parts of Desire: The Hidden World of Islamic Women.* New York: Anchor Books, 1995, p. 32.

later accused of being a puppet of Western powers. His father died three years later.

The young shah ruled Iran together with numerous political groups, from rich landowners to clerics to the Marxist Tudeh Party. The situation was difficult for Mohammad Reza Shah, who seemed to be a weak ruler.[12] In 1949, a man named Mohammad Mossadeq formed the National Front Party, with the goal of upholding the 1906 constitution. Next, he and members of the parliament worked at nationalizing the oil industry, which caused great excitement in Iran. The British were making more money from the Anglo-Iranian Oil Company (AIOC) than was the Iranian government. At the insistence of the people, the shah appointed Mossadeq as prime minister.

Britain removed its technicians and finally imposed a worldwide embargo on the purchase of Iranian oil, which caused oil production to come to a standstill. The British took the case to the International Court of Justice at the Hague, which ruled in favor of Iran. The United States intervened, and the AIOC improved its offer. Friction developed between the shah and Mossadeq as his popularity continued to grow.

When Mossadeq wanted to have the power to appoint the minister of war, the shah refused to grant it, but again, public reaction forced him to change his mind. In 1952, Mossadeq was named *Time* magazine's Man of the Year. He asked for permission to take control of government affairs in Iran and soon reduced the term of the National Assembly from six years to two. Within a year, he had dissolved the legislative body entirely.

U.S. President Dwight D. Eisenhower nurtured (unfounded) concerns that Communists would take over Iran, and in 1953, the United States joined with Great Britain in a plan to overthrow Mossadeq, called Operation Ajax. Kermit Roosevelt, representing the Central Intelligence Agency (CIA), went to Iran to meet with the shah to coordinate the plan. When threatened, Mossadeq refused to step down, and a military coup was set in motion. Mossadeq fled the country, as did the shah, and the newly

Above, Prime Minister Mossadeq arrived in Frankfurt, Germany, in May 1952. Friction developed between Mossadeq and the shah as Mossadeq's popularity grew. In 1953, he was ousted by a military coup orchestrated with the cooperation of the United States and Great Britain.

appointed prime minister, General Fazlollah Zahedi, went into hiding. Meanwhile, riots exploded in the streets between the two groups—those loyal to the shah, and those loyal to Mossadeq. The shah's army prevailed, and Mossadeq was put under house arrest until his death. Hundreds of his followers were put to death, and Mossadeq became a martyr.[13]

It was this event—the ousting of the prime minister—that formed Ebadi's first concrete memory, the year before she started grade school. She and her family were spending the summer with her grandmother in Hamedan. She had been playing games out in the fruit orchards with her cousins. At the end of the day, they rushed into the house to find the adults gathered around the radio. Her grandmother snapped at them to be quiet. A voice on the radio announced that Prime Minister Mohammad Mossadeq had been toppled in a coup d'etat. The actual news meant nothing to the little girl at the time, but the tension that arose in her home from the announcement would always remain with her. At age 57, Ebadi wrote in her memoir, "It was a profoundly humiliating moment for Iranians, who watched the United States intervene in their politics as if their country were some annexed backwater, its leader to be installed or deposed at the whim of an American president and his CIA advisers."[14]

A CHANGE IN THE EBADI FAMILY

For the Ebadi family, as for many others in the country, everything had changed. Ebadi's father was relegated to lower posts, where he had essentially no power. He did not explain to his children why he was home all day, pacing back and forth. He refused to discuss politics in his home from the time of the overthrow on, and he focused instead on raising his children to be technocrats, well-versed in modern technology. As middle-class Iranians, sometimes the financial struggles were felt deeply by the family.

Shirin was fortunate to have a father who treated his daughters the same way he treated his son. Typically, from an early age,

Iranian sons are spoiled by their mothers and numerous female relatives. Girls learn not to question the fact that boys are "more special." This situation only worsens as children grow—the boys' privileges expand while their sisters' contract. When Shirin Ebadi was a child, it was natural for fathers to show more love to their sons than to their daughters. Shirin's father was evenhanded with all three children, however, sometimes to the frustration of his family and staff.

EDUCATION

In 1940, only 10 percent of all elementary-school-age Iranian children were enrolled in school, and fewer than one percent of Iranian teens were enrolled in secondary school.[15] Not until the 1960s did those figures begin to change. This was fortunate for Shirin Ebadi, who loved learning. Young people in Iran during the 1960s were strongly influenced by religious rules and guidance, and the same is true for most Iranian teenagers today. The majority of citizens are Muslims, and their religion is Islam, under which Allah is viewed as both the creator and the master of the world.

Traditionalist Muslims in Iran and other Muslim countries have a strict code of honor and modesty. The sexes tend to be segregated after adolescence, and the relationships of some Muslim girls with nonrelative males are limited at around the age of nine. There are varying degrees of conformity, however, and, as in Western countries, teens follow in their parents' footsteps. Education, social class, lifestyle, and the family's degree of religiousness all play a part in how a child is raised. Ebadi's middle-class family was traditional but not rigidly religious, although they observed the five pillars of Islam: the profession of faith, prayer, almsgiving, fasting during Ramadan, and going on the pilgrimage to Mecca once, if possible, during one's life.[16]

When her older sister married and moved to Hamedan with her husband, Shirin became the eldest at home, which imposed more responsibility on her. Her mother's health was a constant source of anxiety, and Shirin lay awake at night fearing her mother's death. She worried about what would happen to her and her siblings if their mother died. She went up to the attic of their house one day to pray for her mother to live so that she could stay

Influences on the Peacemaker

Ebadi grew up in a democratic household. As an adult she said, "My father's championing of my independence; from the play yard to my later decision to become a judge, instilled a confidence in me that I never felt consciously, but later came to regard as my most valued inheritance."* Her father's mother, Shahrbanu, proved to be a courageous woman when she went to the authorities to insist that she receive what was due her, and was no doubt a role model for Ebadi.

In an interview with Harry Kreisler in May of 2006, Ebadi said that a professor had a profound impact on her. She said, "He was an old man and he was the one who encouraged me to take up the pen and to write. I wrote my first book together with him." She did not mention his name.

But in the end, when asked about her role models, she said,

> I have never been convinced throughout my life that one needs to be imitating others. I even tell my daughters not to look at me as a model. Everyone's condition is different, and the way that each person lives or her life is different. What is important is that one utilizes one's intellect and not to be 100 percent sure about one's convictions. One should always leave room for doubt.**

---

*Harry Kreisler, "The Struggle for Human Rights in Iran: Conversation with Shirin Ebadi." Conversations with History, Institute of International Studies, UC Berkeley. Available at http://globetrotter.berkeley.edu/people6/Ebadi/ebadi-con0.html.
**Ibid.

in school. The custom was for the eldest to take over the household in the event of a mother's death. As she recalled later,

> Suddenly, an indescribable feeling over took me, starting in my stomach and spreading to my fingertips. In that stirring, I felt as though God was answering me. My sadness evaporated, and a strange euphoria shot through my heart. Since that time, my faith in God has been unshakable.[17]

The shah announced the White Revolution in 1963. The intention was to quickly shift the country from an agrarian culture to an industrial one, and the changes were a shock to many of the conservative clerics. Women were given the right to vote. (The shah's position was permanent, but women could vote in the elections for members of parliament.) Just as his father had ordered women to unveil, Mohammad Reza Pahlavi wanted to continue changing the role of women in order to make his country appear more modern. He created prejudice against veiled women by offering better jobs to those who did not wear the veil. According to writer Roksana Bahramitash, women were to "be liberated and serve as cultural transmitters of Western values."[18] The shah and his father could be said to have symbolically created opportunities for women, but in truth their minds were too ingrained by the patriarchal culture to deeply respect women. In an interview with journalist Oriana Fallaci in 1976, Mohammad Reza Shah said,

> I only respect women as long as they are beautiful, feminine, and moderately clever. . . . You (women) are equal in the eyes of the law, but not, excuse my saying so, in ability. . . . You've produced nothing great, nothing![19]

An unprecedented number of women in the urban upper- and middle-class backgrounds entered the workforce. The minimum legal marriage age for women rose to 18, and women's legal rights in divorce and child custody issues improved. The forests were nationalized, a profit-sharing plan for industrial workers created, and a literacy corps founded to eradicate illiteracy in rural areas. Focus was placed on land reform, and some peasants received land of their own.

Ruhollah Khomeini was part of the clergy, and he despised the new changes. He led an uprising that opposed the shah and the White Revolution. Few paid any attention when, in 1964, the same year that Mossadeq died, the shah expelled Khomeini to Najaf, Iraq, because he delivered sermons that attacked the government. The beloved Mossadeq's death rekindled nostalgia and a grief for the Iranian hero-martyr. It also brought up renewed emotional hostility toward America, the country that Iranians continued to blame for his overthrow. With Mossadeq's death, Iranians became more aware of their alienation from their king. In writing about Mossadeq later, Ebadi emphasized the impact that he had on all Iranians—secular and religious, rich and poor. "To them," she wrote in her memoir, *Iran Awakening,* "he was a beloved nationalist hero, a figure worthy of their zealous veneration, a leader fit to guide their great civilization, with its more than 2,500 years of recorded history."[20]

Shiva Balaghi wrote, "To many Iranians, Mossadeq became a symbol of yet another moment in history when foreign intervention played a pivotal role in thwarting a democratic movement in Iran."[21] In addition, the shah's rule grew progressively more repressive as his spending in the name of modernity spiraled out of control. Shirin Ebadi was one of millions whose lives were about to undergo dramatic changes.

CHAPTER 3

Marriage and Revolution

S hirin Ebadi attended two secondary schools, the Anoshiravn Dadgar and Reza Shah Kabir schools, from which she graduated in 1965. At 18, she entered law school at Tehran University, which was founded in 1934. She considered majoring in political science, with the notion of becoming an ambassador, but after thinking about it, she decided she would have a better chance of passing the difficult college examination required to enter the law school. She focused further on becoming a judge, for in Iran a judge is not required to practice law first.

Meanwhile, the city of Tehran began to change rapidly, as the shah, influenced by Western societies, went on a building spree. Nondescript high-rise buildings popped up everywhere. Billboards were plastered with photographs of European starlets, and Western magazines were sold at every kiosk. There were more restaurants and movie theaters—and more slums—than had existed during Ebadi's childhood. The population of the city was about 4 million. It was never a beautiful city, but it had a lot of vitality.

Author Betty Friedan described it in 1975 as looking like "an American Western boom town—buildings going up overnight, international banks next to a Persian Wimpy stand, and no beggars."[22]

Most students at the university were from middle- or working-class backgrounds. They socialized in groups instead of dating individually. Only three women in Ebadi's class wore veils, but the sexes continued to be separated in the classroom: The women sat in the front, and the men in the back. Many traditionalists kept their daughters at home; they had a growing concern that the young people were being too heavily influenced by Western values. The powerful Organization for Intelligence and National Security (SAVAK), an organization of secret police created by the shah, provided enough of a threat to keep them silent.

Shirin Ebadi confronted a whole new set of values as she entered Tehran University. She was slightly shocked by the girls in miniskirts and beehive hairdos. There were also students who felt free to protest practically anything that would not get them arrested. The atmosphere on campus was vibrant, though, and Ebadi soon learned that she was drawn to conflict. She said, "Something about confrontation—perhaps the adrenaline, the spark of an idea, the fleeting sense of agency—appealed to me, and I attended protests regularly."[23] Members of SAVAK were sent to roam the campus, and sometimes were even sent abroad to seek out dissidents if they became too vocal. For Ebadi and her friends, however, SAVAK was a nuisance and not much more.

Ebadi graduated from law school in 1969; she was one of the top two students in her class. She served two years of an internship at the Ministry of Justice, then became a judge in March 1970, at age 23. She was part of the first group of women who entered the system to become judges and was the first to preside over a court.

Although many Iranians grumbled about the excesses and the repression of the shah's regime, Ebadi and her colleagues were not particularly affected. People generally trusted the legal system. It was used by most citizens to deal with everything from divorce to fraud. It was separate from the military courts, where rumors abounded of what happened when dissidents were tried. Ebadi had great respect for the Iranian constitution, and for the rule of law, and it excited her to be a part of the system. In 1971, she received, with honors, a doctorate in private law from Tehran University.

THE SHAH'S PARTY

Over the next eight years, people became more discontented. The clerics were furious about the rapid modernization of their country, which was eroding their power base in the old bazaars (markets) as well as in the villages. The poor, now exposed to television, could see the huge divide between themselves and the rich, and wavered between their desire to consume and their desire to adhere to strict moral codes. Members of the National Front were unhappy with increased repression from the shah. Brown University professor William O. Beeman saw in retrospect that "the civilization had lost its spiritual core. It had become poisoned-obsessed with materialism and the acquisition of money and consumer goods."[24] This situation was particularly difficult for pious Iranians.

In 1971, the shah decided to throw a party to celebrate 2,500 years of the Persian Empire's existence. Presidents and kings from around the world came to Persepolis, the ancient seat of Iran's kings, for an extravaganza that was shocking to Iranians in its blatant display of wealth and ego. The shah had spent $300 million on his party. To the traditionalists, this was an outrage. Ayatollah Khomeini, who had been expelled from Iran in 1963, was a revivalist (one who intentionally revives traditions and makes them into an ideology covering all aspects of life, especially politics). He issued a public criticism of the celebration from Iraq: "It is the kings of Iran that have constantly ordered massacres of their own people. Islam came in order to destroy these palaces of tyranny. Monarchy is one of the most shameful and disgraceful reactionary manifestations."[25] Shirin Ebadi could recall seeing Khomeini on television, but he had not made much of an impression on her.

AN INDEPENDENT WOMAN

One drawback to Ebadi's newfound freedom was that, because of her powerful career, many men did not want to date her. On the other hand, she was well aware that the patriarchal system dominated her culture, and she did not want to fall under the power of a man conditioned to expect submission from a woman. She met Javad Tavassolian, an electrical engineer, in 1975. A neighbor introduced them, and after several meetings, he proposed. Ebadi thought about it, and then suggested that they spend six months getting to know one another, and then not meet again for a month. At that month's end, they could decide what they wanted to do. Her parents were amenable to the idea and would allow them to come and go as they pleased. They separated after six months, and during the one-month hiatus, both knew that they wanted to marry. She was 28 and he was 33. They underwent all the traditional Muslim rites and rituals. His parents drove to her parents' house and asked for Ebadi's hand in marriage, and afterward they gathered in front of the traditional Iranian wedding spread, the *Sofreh Aghd*.[26]

The newly married couple settled into Tavassolian's home in Niavaran, in north Tehran, which was far from the city's center. They eventually moved to Amirabad, to be closer to Ebadi's family. She continued to work, as did most of her female friends who had graduated with her. For a man from a socially conservative background, her new husband was flexible and tolerant. She wrote, "He let me be myself from the beginning, and encouraged my work as a part of me, rather than as a hobby or an indulgence."[27]

U.S. President Jimmy Carter shares a champagne toast with the shah of Iran, above. The event was shown on television, making it the first time that a Muslim nation saw its leader drinking alcohol on television.

OMINOUS MOMENTS

Ebadi recalled finding a leaflet that had been making the rounds in 1977. A trial lawyer, Dariush Forouhar, had taken the words of his beloved Mossadeq and addressed them to the shah. The flyer stated that the shah was overstepping the powers granted to him by the constitution; it also said that he should not interfere with the government's affairs. Ebadi was impressed that someone would have the courage to speak out. Not long afterward, the shah tried to inaugurate the Mediating Council, an extrajudiciary organization that would have adjudicated (judged) cases outside the formal justice system. The shah was trying to reduce the power of the courts. Some of Ebadi's colleagues wrote a letter protesting his action and insisted that all cases had to be tried before the court. Ebadi and many others signed it, as well.

Everyone who signed was threatened with expulsion from court, but nothing came of it.

Then, a series of seemingly minor events began to stir up the political atmosphere. In January 1978, U.S. President Jimmy Carter came to Iran. He and the shah were shown on the televised evening news enjoying a champagne toast. It was the first time a Muslim nation had seen its leader drinking alcohol—forbidden under Islam—on television. The irony was that Jimmy Carter was a strong Baptist, and himself drank only on rare occasions. In response, seminarians marched on the shrine in the holy city of Qom, demanding Ayatollah Khomeini's return from Iraq. The shah's police shot into the crowd, killing several protestors. Ayatollah Khomeini let his fury be known from Iraq.

Ebadi was not particularly shocked by these events. The mosque traditionally was known as a place where grievances could be aired in a protective atmosphere. In addition, it was not that uncommon for the mullahs to intervene. Then, 400 people were burned alive at a cinema in Abadan, in the south. The shah blamed religious conservatives, and Khomeini retaliated by accusing the SAVAK. Until then, the population had seemed ambivalent. The two warring factions—the clergy and the shah—caused people to sit up and take note. Resentments of the shah, the rich, and the United States had been festering for years among the traditionalists. Many had come to believe that anything would be better than what they had. The clerics railed against the shah in their sermons. Riots in Qom, a deeply conservative area, touched off another volley of mourning and protests in 1978.

Workers began to strike. Street demonstrations raged out of control, and the shah's prime minister, Jafar Sharif-Emami, sent in tanks to disperse the people in Zhaleh Square. When that tactic failed, soldiers were ordered to shoot into the crowd. About 600 demonstrators were killed, and the day became known as Black Friday.[28]

Months before, the frustrated shah had asked Saddam Hussein to expel Khomeini from Najaf, to decrease the influence he

When Ayatollah Ruhollah Khomeini (above) was expelled from Iraq, France was willing to offer him asylum. He moved to a town west of Paris and continued his influence on the people of Iran through telephone and audio cassette messages.

had on the masses in Iran, and Hussein agreed. Khomeini was refused entry to Kuwait, but France was willing to take him. He moved and began to issue orders from the house he rented in Neauphle-le-Château, a town 25 miles from Paris. He insisted that the shah leave Iran. As much as he spoke for the people, Khomeini surely had not forgotten that the shah had jailed him for his opposition to the plans to redistribute land to the peasants, grant voting rights to women, and shield members of the American armed forces from criminal prosecution in Iranian courts.[29]

Khomeini was a charismatic leader, and he also knew how to manipulate the masses. He could describe the people's objectives for them and define the enemies of Islam. In Iran, those enemies included anyone who did not share the clerics' interpretation of Islam or who imported artifacts of Western civilization, which were thought to be causing Islam to founder. Khomeini's was the first electronic revolution. He directed his followers by telephone from France, using the direct dialing that the shah had brought to Iran. He made cassettes and sent them with followers who were headed back to Iran. They made copies and distributed them, so that millions of people could hear Khomeini's words.[30]

WHAT ABOUT THE WOMEN?

Women from rural areas were on the margins of society; they did not expect to have a voice. As antagonism developed between the clerics and the shah, however, they became more critical of the shah. They, too, felt that their culture was disappearing. An Islamic writer and political activist named Ali Shariati published a book about the daughter of the Prophet Muhammad, portraying her as a strong-willed woman who stood by her husband in their struggle to achieve justice. Many educated Iranian women related to her and, in a kind of solidarity, began to wear their own version of hijab, composed of a headscarf, long coat, trousers, and running shoes.

On January 16, 1979, the shah of Iran fled the country with his family. They are shown here during a stay in the Bahamas in April of that year. In the end, they remained in permanent exile.

This was great news for the Ayatollah Khomeini; the women were playing directly into his hands. From Paris, he instructed the people of Iran to expel the shah's ministers from their offices. The fervor surrounding the possibility of ousting the shah was contagious, and Ebadi was no exception. She asked herself: "Who did I have more in common with, in the end: an opposition led by mullahs who spoke in the tones familiar to ordinary Iranians or the gilded court of the shah, whose officials cavorted with American starlets at parties soaked in expensive American champagne?"[31] This was the attitude of millions of middle-class women in Tehran. Still, no one could believe they were in the center of a burgeoning revolution. Was it possible that the people could overturn the government they had come to despise? The notion was thrilling.

There were the naysayers, of course. These included an elder judge, who confronted Ebadi. "You of all people," he said, "Why are you here? Don't you know that you're supporting people who will take away your job if they come to power?" Ebadi replied, "I'd rather be a free Iranian than an enslaved attorney!"[32] She, and many like her, however, had not read Khomeini's book entitled *Islamic Government,* basically a collection of lectures he had delivered in 1970. He made it clear even then that the religious expert should be occupying himself with government affairs, and that in an Islamic government, there was little room for opinions.

The country was in chaos, and anyone could see that Khomeini was winning the battle. The opportunists came forward, many of them deciding to switch allegiances when they realized that the current government would not stand up under the protests. On January 16, 1979, the shah fled Iran with his family, leaving the country in the hands of his prime minister, Shahpour Bakhtiar. At the airport, the shah broke down and cried when his officers took his hands and kissed them. He had in his possession a small box of Iranian soil and hundreds of pieces of luggage. He later learned that he had cancer.[33]

The citizens of Iran broke out fits of joy and celebration. Ebadi and her family were elated, too. They felt that they had "reclaimed a dignity that, until recently, many of us had not even realized we had lost."[34] Once the shah departed, Ayatollah Khomeini, who had been in exile for 17 years, was ready to move in. On February 1, 1979, the ayatollah, left his wife behind, and boarded an Air France Boeing 747 jet headed for Tehran—if it was allowed to land or was not shot down when it arrived. He brought along with him 47 of his closest male followers, a volunteer crew, and 141 journalists.[35]

CHAPTER 4

New Baby and Second Revolution

When the 78-year-old stern-faced Ayatollah Khomeini disembarked from his plane on February 1, he was met by millions of jubilant supporters. During his exile in France, he had ignited a revolution that would later be compared to the French and Russian revolutions of past centuries. Ignoring the tanks and military vehicles that shot at his followers, Khomeini appointed Mehdi Bazargan as prime minister of the provisional government four days after he returned to Iran. Over the next month, he invited the shah's army to join him. They held their ground. An emergency military government was set up in every town to try to curb the rioting. The crowds were frenzied and out of control, which worked in Ayatollah Khomeini's favor. In an attempt to heighten the zeal of the people, he told all citizens to "go up to their rooftops at 9:00 P.M. and scream *Allahu akbar,* 'God is greatest.'"[36]

He knew how to play the crowd, Ebadi thought, but she and her family happily joined in. The cries could be heard all over the

When Ayatollah Khomeini took power in 1979, a special referendum was held to ask Iranians if they wished to become an Islamic republic—98 percent said yes. Above, women hold up pictures of the ayatollah during a 2006 demonstration to protest against nonobservance of Islamic dress codes in Iran.

city—one mass voice of solidarity. The military set a curfew, warning people to be in their houses by 4:00 P.M., but the ayatollah told the people to come out into the streets. Finally, the shah's army split apart and announced its neutrality. After 2,500 years, the monarchy of Iran had been abolished. Citizens had been assured that Iran's Islamic Republic would allow them to live in peace. In a special referendum, Iranians were asked if they wanted to become an Islamic Republic; 98 percent said yes. Many political organizations objected on the grounds that people did not have any chance of expressing their ideas, but to no avail. In March 1979, the Islamic Republic of Iran was born.

Khomeini created the Supreme Council of the Islamic Revolution, and members went right to work to organize a new government. They drafted a constitution using some of the articles of the abolished 1906 constitution and borrowing from the French constitution written under Charles de Gaulle in 1958. Elections were held for the Council of Experts, but new laws prevented small, radical groups from being represented. Political groups again objected and were ignored. When their objections were published, Khomenei simply closed down the offending publications.

Little was mentioned about the political role of the clergy, but when the constitution was presented to the Council of experts, which was dominated by Shia clergy, some representatives were dissatisfied with the secular nature of the new document; they revised it to make it more Islamic. It was soon clear that Khomeini wanted to create a radical new interpretation of Shiism, the religion of 90 percent of Iranians. Bazargan soon resigned, and the ayatollah, with his newly created doctrine known as the *Velayat-e-Faqih* ("rule by jurisprudence"), had more power than the shah ever had. For Ebadi and others, it was time to reexamine the man who would go down in history as the only person who had ever combined political and religious authority as a head of state.

(continues on page 36)

Fundamentalism

The term *fundamentalism* dates back to an early twentieth-century American religious movement that took its name from a series of books published by Protestant laymen entitled *The Fundamentals: A Testimony of Truth.* Millions of copies were circulated. The original fundamentalist movement was basically a religious revival, but it expanded into the political and social life of its followers. In the Middle East, the rise of fundamentalism, also called revivalism, came before the Iranian Revolution. The Arab defeat in the 1967 war with Israel marked a time when Muslims became disillusioned with borrowed ideologies and cultures. People in the Islamic states of the Middle East wanted to restore Islam to a central role in political and social life.

Much of fundamentalism, or revivalism, has to do with change. Some embrace it, but when it is imposed on others, they sometimes react violently, especially when they believe that their power and authority are being usurped. Leaders of these kinds of movements believe that internal decadence could be the cause, and they accuse members of becoming weak. This, in turn, leads to physical and mental training programs to strengthen the character and resolve of those who want to restore the group to its former, idealized state.

The group advocates violence to ward off oppressors. (American fundamentalists reacted violently, for example, after abortion was legalized.) According to Karen Armstong in her book entitled *Islam,*

> All fundamentalist movements have in common a disenchantment with the modern experiment, which has not fulfilled all that it promised, an expression of real fear, where members are convinced that the secular movement is determined to wipe religion out. All are often radical in their reinterpretation of religion. All are highly critical of democracy and secularism.*

Modern Islamic revivalist movements have usually shared these basic tenets:

1. Because Islam is a comprehensive religion and way of life, it can point to a "right" form of politics, law, and society.
2. The problems of Muslim societies are a result of people trying to follow a Western, secular way of life, which is seen as materialistic.
3. Islamic law should replace all Western civil code brought in by colonial powers.
4. Modernization without Westernization is quite possible, that is, science and technology can be reconciled with religious values.
5. Muslims need to organize and dedicate themselves to struggle (jihad) against immoral and unjust practices. Radical activists have called for the use of force to implement the above tenets.**

The modern "Islamic movement" actually began around 1875. After colonization in the Middle East, leaders began to idealize the centuries before "occupation." Jamal al-Din al-Afghani was an important originator of today's Muslim revivalist thought. He hated the corruption he saw all around him. He believed that Muslims could improve their societies by reinterpreting Islamic texts through fresh eyes and by searching for ways to fight colonial rule and make their politics and culture independent of the West. In the eyes of many Muslims, the Iranian Revolution of 1979 is considered to be a successful fundamentalist revival.

---

*Beeman, William O., "Fighting the Good Fight: Fundamentalism and Religious Revival." In J. MacClancy, ed. *Anthropology for the Real World*. Chicago: University of Chicago Press, 2001.

**Esposito, John L., *Islam: The Straight Path*. Oxford, U.K.: Oxford Univerity Press, 1988. p. 169–170.

(continued from page 33)

RUHOLLAH MUSAVI KHOMEINI

Khomeini was born in the town of Khomein, about 200 miles south of Tehran. His father, the chief Shia cleric of the town, was murdered when Ruhollah was an infant. The boy was raised by his mother and his aunt. From an early age, he was trained in Islamic studies. He had an older brother who was an ayatollah in the city of Qom. When Ruhollah was a teenager, his mother and his aunt died. He moved to Qom, married, and had two sons and three daughters. He had always believed that it was right for clerics to be politically active. One of his early books, *Discovery of Secrets,* disputed the outspoken advocacy of secularism in the 1940s. In a later book, he rejected the Iranian constitution and the monarchy. He believed the supreme religious leader, or *faqih,* should be in charge of the Muslim community, called the *umma.* In 1962, Khomeini led an uprising against the shah and was exiled to Iraq. The shah's White Revolution in 1963 sparked Khomeini's ire once again, and he made a commitment over the next 16 years to return to Iran to set things right.

A NEW VERSION OF ISLAM

In Islam, God, or Allah, is the supreme head of state, the source of authority and law. According to Bernard Lewis,

> The state is God's law, the law is God's law. The army is God's law—and of course the enemy is God's enemy. Those who exercise authority do so on behalf of God, in the same way and perhaps to the same extent as the prime minister of England exercises authority on behalf of the Queen and the president of the United States on behalf of the people.[37]

The Koran is a moral rule book. Islamic doctrine is basically egalitarian (everyone is treated equally), although it is limited to free adult male Muslims. That was an advance, however, on the practices of the Greco-Roman and the ancient Iranian worlds.

Religion has a different meaning for Muslims and Westerners; in the West it occupies only one compartment of life, as we tend to classify by nation, country, and other subdivisions. Muslims find their basic identity and loyalty in the religious community. Islam is also the only acceptable basis for authority. In Islam, there is no distinction between church and state. In the West, church and state are separate.

Muslims have two different definitions of Islam. One is a legalistic and absolutist Islam. The other is a pluralistic and tolerant Islam that combines modern democratic ideals.[38] Shirin Ebadi subscribes to the latter. Iftikhar Ahmad wrote about her:

> Ebadi represents a pacifist, pluralist, and tolerant Islam. She says that her interpretation is pacifist because she believes that Islam is a religion of peace and that Islamic values are compatible with the values of universal human rights. Her notion of Islam is pluralist because she believes that Islam is respectful of diverse faiths and that it teaches gender equality, social justice, and democratic living. She believes that Islam teaches respect for life, liberty, justice, social justice, gender equality, and human dignity.[39]

Iran needed a new president, and in January 1980, Abolhassan Bani-Sadr, Khomeini's choice, was elected, after many tactics had been used to reduce the number of challengers. By summer, all political groups opposed to Khomeini and his changes were forced to go underground. The Revolutionary Guard and other groups were established and allowed to violently attack the opposition.

WOMEN UNDER FIRE AGAIN

As Khomeini forged his new political system, women came under fire for not meeting the approval of men. The emancipation of women is a hallmark of Western culture, so the leaders of the growing fundamentalist movement felt obligated to get women back into the home, and in many areas, back under the veil. It was as if one man was turning the clock back more than 1,000 years. Women of all persuasions had banded together to rid their country of the shah, but now they would more than likely be divided again. Some succumbed to the demands of the clergy; others rebelled against the new, strictly enforced dress code. More important, however, they were divided in their reaction toward the new laws that would eliminate any freedom they had gained.

THE PERSONAL AND THE POLITICAL

Ebadi had suffered two miscarriages and had made an appointment with a medical specialist in New York before the revolution. Somehow, she managed to receive special permission from the deputy prime minister to leave the country, and she and her husband left in April. They were gone from Iran for a month, and on their return, the changes shocked them. Streets had been renamed. When Ebadi went to the justice offices, she was shocked to see that the men were not wearing suits and ties but collarless shirts and plain slacks. It was suddenly politically correct to look poor in order to identify with the masses. It was rumored that women could no longer be judges. The world as Ebadi knew it no longer existed. Soon, she learned she was pregnant.

Fathollah Bani-Sadr, the brother of the president, was appointed provisional overseer of the Ministry of Justice. Ebadi and several colleagues went to congratulate him. She was secretly hoping that she would receive a word of praise for her work for the revolution; after all, she had won a battle, too. Instead, he said, "Don't you think that out of respect for our beloved Imam Khomeini, who has graced Iran with his return, it would be better if you covered your hair?"[40]

Under the new penal code introduced in 1980, women were made subservient to men in myriad ways. Nonetheless, many Iranian women appeared to support the regime under Ayatollah Khomeini. In this photograph from 1979, a young girl holds a portrait of the leader during regular prayer services.

WOMEN AND THE NEW PENAL CODE

One day while at work, Ebadi picked up a newspaper and read a draft of the Islamic penal code. She was shocked, as she knew that it would "fundamentally transform the very basis of governance, the relationship of citizens to laws, the organizing principles and social contracts along which society is conducted."[41]

She understood that the value of a woman's life was now half that of a man's (if a couple were hit by a car on the street, the cash compensation due to the woman's family was half that due to the man's). A woman from then on would have to ask her husband's permission for a divorce, and if she testified in court about a crime she had witnessed, her testimony counted only half as much as a man's. Even more, women were to be veiled, and if they disobeyed, they would be lashed. Ebadi could not live by such laws. It particularly infuriated her that her husband had so much control over her, power granted to him by a group of men. She decided that a postnuptial agreement might be in order; her husband could sign a paper granting her the right to divorce him, and giving her primary custody of their children in the event they did not stay together. He completely agreed with the idea.

EDUCATION

The sexes were completely segregated again under the new law, which legitimized the entry of millions of lower-class girls from traditional families and rural areas into the public life and the education system. Fathers who had prevented their daughters from attending school were encouraged to send them off. Conflicts arose, however, between students who wanted a thorough desecularization of administrations, faculties, and curricula, and students who wanted to retain a secular system. Violent clashes occurred at several universities in 1979 and 1980.[42] The government's answer was to close all 200 institutions of higher learning. Professors and students who disagreed with the new government regulations were purged, and many were killed. When the colleges reopened, only a fraction of students returned. At Ebadi's alma mater, the University of Tehran, student enrollment declined from 17,000 to 4,500.

Ebadi was warned that a purging committee might be formed at her office. Bani-Sadr, the justice minister, came to Ebadi and suggested that she be transferred to the investigative office of the ministry. She was still clinging to her judgeship, and she worried that people would think the rank of judgeship was closing to women. She rejected the prestigious job. Bani-Sadr told her that, if a purging committee came in, she could be demoted to court assistant. She stood her ground. She was the most distinguished female judge in the court system, and she had lent her name to the revolution. Surely they would not demote her. The woman who had been brought up in an apolitical household was feeling the fire of rebellion that would come to be her trademark in the future.

THE SIEGE OF THE AMERICAN EMBASSY

Iranians began to adjust to the strict lifestyle imposed on them, and to a government that many feared would be worse than the one they had before. In November 1979, a group of students who called themselves the Followers of the Path of the Imam Khomeini seized the U.S. Embassy and took 52 staff members hostage.

Ebadi was expecting a baby the following April. She worried constantly that the United States would attack at any moment. Surely Khomeini would command the group of radical youngsters to release the hostages. He did the opposite, however: He praised their courage and called their hostile act a second revolution. The Islamic Republic of Iran was only nine months old and was already involved in an international crisis. Ebadi, along with many of her friends and associates, was horrified. Did the radicals think that such an act meant that they had defeated America? The students quickly became heroes. Khomeini used the occasion to list his demands from the United States: He wanted the shah returned to Iran. He demanded an apology from the United States for its involvement in Iran, including the coup that overthrew Mossadeq, and he wanted a promise that America would stay out of Iran's business.

To the amazement of the Iranians, the United States did not attack. Instead, the U.S. government announced that it would freeze Iranian assets in the United States, which included billions of dollars, and would halt oil imports. In April 1980, a U.S. mission to rescue the hostages was aborted after a sandstorm caused damage to eight helicopters. The United States was thoroughly humiliated. Secretary of State Cyrus Vance resigned. The Iranian

In November 1979, a group of students loyal to Ayatollah Khomeini seized the U.S. Embassy in Tehran, taking 52 staff members hostage. In this photograph, one of the hostages, blindfolded and with his hands bound, is displayed to the crowd gathered outside the embassy.

students, gaining in confidence, went through the files of the embassy and announced Iranians who had allegedly spied for the American government. Each name that was read signified the death of another Iranian citizen.

People gathered around the embassy. They shouted slogans like "Death to America!" The atmosphere became that of a circus. People took their babies in strollers, and food vendors lined up. At the same time, leaders of countries all over the world showed up to plead with Khomeini to release the hostages. Even the pope sent an envoy, but Khomeini sent back a rhetorical reply, "Where was the pope when our young people were being tortured in the shah's prisons?"[43]

In July 1980, Reza Shah died in Egypt, which eased the tensions between the United States and Iran somewhat. The standoff went on for 444 days, however, and would affect politics in both counties for many years to come. President Jimmy Carter was defeated in the next election. On January 20, 1981, the day of Ronald Reagan's inauguration, the hostages were released. The United States unfroze almost $8 billion in Iranian funds in America and agreed that the hostages would not be able to sue Iran. Economic sanctions remained in place.

After Reagan's election, allegations were made that William Casey, Ronald Reagan's campaign director, secretly met with Iranian officials in Europe before Reagan was in office to arrange for the hostages' release. Bani-Sadr wrote in his memoir, "I have proof of contacts between Khomeini and the supporters of Ronald Regan as early as the spring of 1980."[44] Gary Sick, who had been President Carter's principal aide on Iran, gave details in his book, entitled *October Surprise*, of meetings between Iranian hardliners and Republican Party officials. William Casey, who was Reagan's campaign manager and later his CIA chief, was a part of the meetings.[45] These claims have never been proven, but they have not been refuted, either.

Ebadi gave birth on April 21, 1980, to a girl named Negar. For two months, she stayed home with her baby, a wonderful temporary respite from strife and uncertainty. When the time came for her to return to work, Ebadi left Negar with the baby's grandmother. The ministry was filled with her colleagues who lived every day in fear of being branded anti-Islamic. It was a time of great uncertainty and disappointment, but for most, the only choice they had was to live from day to day.

CHAPTER 5

Iran at War With Iraq

n September 1980, Saddam Hussein of Iraq invaded Iran. He had felt threatened by Ayatollah Khomeini's revolution and by the call Khomeini put out to Muslims all over the world to rise up against their secular governments. Because the majority of citizens in Iraq were Shia, like Khomeini, Hussein had reason to worry. Hussein had always wanted to redraw the borders and take over the oil-rich Iran, so the slightest provocation was bound to get a reaction. For his part, Khomeini had made it known that he was determined to spread his radical, political Shiism far and wide. In fact, the Iranian revolutionaries envisioned a Shia uprising that would erase the boundaries created by the British. On September 22, Hussein's troops occupied a 30-mile swath of Iranian land. The two leaders faced off. Hussein declared himself the regional leader; after all, the Koran was written in Arabic. Khomeini called it a war between "Islam and blasphemy."[46]

Sadly, Khomeini had no problem sending young men onto the battlefields as foot soldiers. He had to figure out a way to get them to volunteer for the front, however. So, he promised them a "short-cut to Heaven." The young soldiers, some in their teens, could be seen on television, wearing red bandannas, with their keys to heaven around their necks, carrying small Korans and pictures of Ayatollah Khomeini and Imam Ali, the first Shia *imam*.[47] The boys were sent to battle in front of the older soldiers, across minefields.

The spirit of martyrdom was strong under the guidance of Khomeini; it was a spirit that dated back to Imam Hossein of the seventh century, who martyred himself for his people. Khomeini told the young that martyrdom was a perfect death. One young man told an interviewer that "The Koran says, 'Those who die for God are martyrs, and the martyrs never die. They live forever.'"[48] The story of Imam Hossein defending his family and friends at the Battle of Karbala was reenacted every year to keep the spirit of martyrdom fresh in the minds of the people. Khomeini also claimed that God had commanded the war, and a strong sense of nationalism rose up in the Iranians. Therefore, Khomeini was let off the hook for demanding sacrifices of his people.

Saddam Hussein had the advantage in this war, according to Ebadi, because "he was purchasing chemical agents from Western European firms and stores of weaponry from the United States."[49] In 1984, he used chemical weapons against the Iranians. He started with sarin, then switched to mustard gas. Both caused horrible symptoms that killed the victims or left them ill for life. Iran made many appeals to the United Nations, to no avail. The world watched and did nothing.

Joyce Battle, a Middle East analyst at the National Security Archive at George Washington University, was interviewed in 2003 about the Iran–Iraq War. A series of declassified U.S. documents posted on the Web detail the United States' backing of Saddam Hussein. The administration had received a report indicating that Iraq was using chemical weapons against Iran and against Iraqi Kurds in the early 1980s. That did not prevent the United States from providing intelligence and military assistance to Iraq, according to Battle. She stated emphatically that the United States should have done more to end the war, and she agreed with Ebadi that too many countries had "ulterior motives and did not do enough to cut off arms shipments to the two combatants."[50]

Sunni and Shia

At the age of 40 (in A.D. 610), a tribesman named Muhammad ibn Abdullah began to hear verses in Arabic that would become the *Quran*, or Koran ("recitation"). It is the equivalent of the Bible for Christians. He began to preach to a community of believers, and they called their religion Islam. Some of the leaders in his homeland of Mecca became hostile, however, and Muhammad's clan was censured. Muhammad did the unthinkable for that time—he turned his back on his tribe and moved to another place, called Yathrib. There, he formed a community that attracted people who came together because of their beliefs rather than because of family ties.

Yathrib would become known as Medina, or "the City," because it was a perfect Muslim society. After the Prophet Muhammad died, Muslims had to decide how to continue. Some thought the Prophet would have wanted to be succeeded by his closest male relative, Ali ibn Abi Talib. Others thought that each tribal group should elect its own *imam,* or leader. Finally it was decided that one of the Prophet's followers, not a relative, should head the community. A man named Abu Bakr was elected. He turned out to be a good leader, and so was his successor, Umar ibn al-Khattab, who led his people in raids on non-Muslim communities in Syria, Iraq, Egypt, and the Persian Empire. Before long, he and his warriors had created a vast empire that stretched from the Pyrenees to the Himalayas, where they managed to live harmoniously with the people they conquered.

The third leader, Uthman, was murdered by soldiers committing mutiny. His death divided the Muslims, which was the beginning of the Sunni–Shia disagreement. Ali ibn Abi Talib, who

DISMISSAL

In Iran, a law was passed that forbade women to be judges. At the end of 1980, Shirin Ebadi was called to a meeting where a group of men sat at a table. She was told to show up at the legal office when her vacation was over. She knew what it meant: She was being

was the Prophet Muhammad's cousin and also married to the Prophet's daughter, became the fourth leader. He agreed with those who thought Uthman's killers were carrying out a just and necessary task and should be protected. For this idea, Ali was murdered in A.D. 661, and the power swung back to the group of Umayyad, to which Uthman had belonged.

Those who sided with the Umayyad were eventually called the Sunnis, from the word *Sunna*, which in Arabic means "tradition" or "custom." Those siding with Ali came to be called *Shia* (meaning "partisans" or "followers"). An even more decisive split between Sunni and Shia happened in A.D. 680, when Ali's group urged Ali's son, Hussein, to rise up against the Umayyad authorities. Hussein was hoping to bring Muslims back under the authority of the Prophet Muhammad's descendants, thought by Shia to be divinely inspired and infallible *imams.* Hussein was brutally killed, however, by the army of Yazid, who was the Umayyad caliph. Hussein became a martyr for the Shia population.

The two main branches of Islam have always agreed on the five pillars of the faith, but have disagreed over delegation of power and authority within the religion, much in the same way that Protestants and Catholics have disagreed within Christianity. Sunnis (like many Protestants) are more likely to follow their own readings of religious texts than Shias, who, like many Catholics, are more inclined to listen to priests or other religious leaders. Both Sunnis and Shias claim the Prophet Muhammad to be their model, and both can and do worship together without any problems, much as Protestants and Catholics might do. In the Muslim world today, which includes nearly a billion followers of Islam from many different ethnic backgrounds, Sunnis are the majority; Shias are the minority, at roughly 15 percent.

demoted to a clerk or perhaps a typist, which made her furious.[51] She thought about it and decided that she was not going to let them get the better of her. She went to the legal office, explained what had happened to her, and declared that she would continue to come to the office, but she was not going to do her work. Her boss, who had known her before, let her be. She was also glad she had said no to Bani-Sadr's offer to work as a counselor in the president's office, for she could see how the revolutionaries were reinventing their standards every day. (The man who did accept the job was eventually executed by firing squad, and the president was removed from office.)

The living rooms of Iranian homes were filled with televised images of violence. There was a revolution and a war occurring simultaneously. People saw on television or read in their newspapers about former dissidents being hanged every day. So many were executed that people began to make jokes about it, in order to hold onto their sanity. Author Bernard Lewis described the situation:

> The summary trial and execution of great numbers of ideologically defined enemies; the driving into exile of hundreds of thousands of men and women; the large-scale confiscation of private property; the mixture of repression and subversion; the violence and indoctrination that accompanied the consolidation of power-these methods can hardly be called Islamic; they are, however, thoroughly revolutionary.[52]

Most of the shah's soldiers, who had been jailed, were released to help fight the enemy. Food was rationed. No one wanted to voice their despair while the war was raging. The ayatollah once again needed the support of everyone, especially the women. He announced a series of *jihads*, or "struggles," that needed to occur. He pronounced a jihad against foreign invasion, a jihad against illiteracy, and another against the possibility of a coup. He commanded the women to have more children. Women were now seen as active citizens of the republic. Now that literacy was a religious duty, millions of women started learning how to read, and they put heart and soul into building the economy and winning the war. They raised money, and there were outreach programs to help the poor. The Iranian women were determined to free their country from domination of other countries. Unfortunately, their dedication and generosity was not returned. Many women, unable to support themselves and their children while their husbands were at war, turned to prostitution; others turned to drugs.[53]

THE MKO

Problems continued in Iran. A faction called the Mojahedin-e Khalgh Organization (MKO) was at odds with Khomeini. They, too, had opposed the Pahlavi monarchy, but theirs was a more socialist, militant reading of Islam. Their ideology appealed to the educated middle class, who were moderately religious. Sociologist and writer Ali Shariati took a leading role in this faction. He revived the tradition of making heroes out of the seventh-century Shia characters Imam Ali and Fatemeh, Muhammad's daughter. The philosophy he espoused was more about resistance than defeat. He was persuasive, but millions of Iranians chose Khomeini's fundamentalist Islam over Shariati's secular leftism. He and his followers had helped to propel the revolution, but Khomeini, when he took over, dismissed the MKO because it was too competitive. Members of the MKO were among the radical groups that were forced to go underground in 1981 because they opposed Khomeini's government. They continued to conduct regular attacks against revolutionary officials and buildings, however.

In 1982, a series of particularly bloody battles in the port city of Khorramshahr divided Iraq and Iran. In the end, Iranian soldiers took 12,000 Iraqis prisoner. One hundred thousand Iranian soldiers had been killed, and the people felt certain the war would now end. The most radical members of the ayatollah's followers had a dream of conquering ancient Mesopotamia, however. They wanted the ayatollah to push forward to Baghdad to unseat Saddam Hussein.

The situation was becoming more frightening every day. Not only were young soldiers dying in waves, but anyone suspected of sympathizing with leftist groups like the MKO was put before a firing squad. The ayatollah declared a purge of any literature that could feed the wrong message to the masses. Ebadi pulled books by Marx and Lenin and others off her shelves and burned them. Her husband invited his 17-year-old brother, Fuad, to come and stay with them; he was attracted to the MKO and had even started to sell their booklets at his school. Ebadi liked him and admired the way he had not retreated inside, the way the rest of them had. Her husband worried, though, and with good reason.

While walking along the street, Ebadi's brother-in-law was arrested. His mother managed to get in touch with the prime minister, who told her that her son would have to recant his views and cooperate with the regime. He was sentenced to 20 years in prison. He refused to cooperate by "naming names" and renouncing all political affiliations. They broke his jaw, then his arm. When his father was killed in a car accident, Fuad was allowed to leave prison to attend the funeral. He told his family that he wanted to escape, but they were certain he would go back to the MKO. His relatives watched him, and then delivered him back to prison.

HITTING ROCK BOTTOM

Another girl, Nargess, was born to Ebadi and her husband in 1983. A year later, Ebadi applied for retirement from the ministry. She would receive benefits. She was 35 years old, and she had worked for 15 years. She watched as women who were once her colleagues bowed to the authority of the clerics and accepted the clerical jobs. Ebadi's husband was working as an electrical engineer. It was a difficult time, emotionally and financially. Then another blow came. The authorities shut down the company at which Ebadi's husband had been working, claiming that it was filled with Communists. Ebadi's family had little money, and expenses were high.

In 1986, a scandal erupted when a Lebanese newspaper claimed that the United States had agreed to sell Iran missiles in exchange for American hostages who had been captured in Lebanon. The profit was being sent to the Contras in South America, where the U.S. government was trying to influence politics. Not only was the exchange illegal, but American citizens were horrified to learn that weapons had been sold to the enemy. It made the Iranians, on the other hand, question the "fiery anti-American stance" of their leaders.[54]

Iranians began to leave their country in droves. They went to Europe and the United States to start new lives. This resulted in a huge brain drain (intellectuals leaving the country). The Islamic Republic of Iran was tearing families apart, and people's bitterness grew. Ebadi was sad and angry. She found herself going to the homes of her friends, sometimes pleading, and sometimes defying them to leave. She took one trip to India with her family, but they were so terrified of being bombed that they did not leave Iran again. Ebadi wrote, "Time passed in drips."[55]

In 1988, Iraq began to launch missiles at Tehran, and Ebadi and her family grew strangely accustomed to the noise. The war was in their backyards. The wealthier citizens moved into hotels that could withstand the attacks. Tehran was not obliterated, but many parts of the city were destroyed. Ebadi's day finally came when a bomb landed close enough to throw her against the concrete side of a building. Her husband was frightened and insisted that they move to northern Iran, near the Caspian Sea. She would not leave her parents, who refused to go, so finally her husband stayed, and Ebadi and her two daughters went to the north.

In July 1988, Ebadi turned on the television and saw that a U.S. warship in the Persian Gulf had fired at an Iranian civilian airplane, killing all 290 people on board. The United States, still under the presidency of Ronald Reagan, claimed that the ship's crew had mistaken the plane for an Iranian fighter plane. Many wondered if the United States would openly join Saddam Hussein and annihilate Iran. The United Nations Security Council called for a cease-fire resolution, and Hussein and Khomeini decided, after eight years and the loss of 500,000 lives, to accept.

Most of the war had been fought on Iranian soil, and the farmland, cities, economy, and industry were all devastated. For Ayatollah Khomieni, his dream of universal revolution through-out the Muslim world was over. Iraq's Shia majority would not become a satellite state of Iran. Most appalling to Ebadi was that nothing had changed. She wondered who had won and came to the conclusion that it was the arms dealers, the "European com-panies that sold Saddam his chemical weapons, the American firms that sold both sides arms. They amassed fortunes."[56] In the meantime, half a million lives had been lost.

A LIFE-CHANGING MOMENT

Meanwhile, the MKO had been busy. Not even a week after the war ended, they sent 7,000 fighters over from training grounds in Iraq to attack Kermanshah, a city in Iran. Their goal was to bring down Iran's government. They called the attack Eternal Light. They were certain that the Iranian people would see what they were doing and join them. It was a tragic mistake. The Iranian people were furious with them for joining Saddam's army, and furthermore, they could not handle any more violence.

This was terrible timing for Ebadi's brother-in-law Fuad, who was wasting away in prison. In the fall of 1988, Ebadi received the call they had been dreading. Fuad, 24 years old, had been executed. Ebadi could not stop thinking that this young man had been put to death for selling newspapers, after serving seven years of a long prison sentence. Ebadi said, "That night, a mute fury settled in my stomach. When I think back and try to pinpoint the moment that changed me, the moment when my life took a dif-ferent course, I see that it all began that night."[57]

CHAPTER 6

Rebel
With
a Cause

After Fuad's murder, Ebadi learned that she had high blood pressure. Her husband, Javad, developed asthma. They had been told by the authorities not to discuss Fuad's death. The furious and devastated Ebadi instead began to tell anyone who would listen about his death. Ebadi was always the first to acknowledge that she was rebellious and stubborn. Both traits were evident in this new crisis. It did not occur to her that she might be risking her life. What she did know was that the interior pain was so great that she had to do something. During the funeral held for Fuad's father, the mourners also grieved his young son. Ebadi stood, numb with grief, wishing that they had allowed him to run away on that fateful day.

On June 3, 1989, Ebadi turned on the television and heard the Koran being recited without pause. She knew that Ayatollah Khomeini was dead. Millions of Iranians dressed in black moved through the city, wailing in the traditional Shia way. Seyyed Ali Khamenei became the new supreme spiritual leader; he was elected by the Assembly of Experts.

Salman Rushdie: A Shocking Fatwa

In 1989, Ayatollah Khomeini issued a *fatwa,* or religious edict, against Salman Rushdie, because in his novel, *The Satanic Verses,* Rushdie had insulted the Prophet Muhammad. Rushdie, an Indian Muslim who was living in London at the time, was accused of blasphemy, a serious crime, but added to that was the accusation of apostasy, or abandoning Islam, which in militant Islamic Law deserves death. Khomeini's ruling was based on a saying by the Prophet Muhammad that is accepted only by the Shiites and a small minority of Sunnis in Central Asia: "If anyone insults me, then any Muslim who hears him must kill him immediately, without any need to refer to the imam or the sultan." Most people would take that to mean that, if an insult occurred spontaneously, then perhaps there was a reason to punish the person, but nothing is mentioned about an arranged killing. Furthermore, with Sharia, as in any system of law, there needs to be an accused and an accuser, a verdict, and a sentence. This was not the case with Rushdie.

In 1989, Ayatollah Khomeini issued a fatwa, or religious edict, directing Muslims to kill author Salman Rushdie because he had insulted the Prophet Muhammad. Since then, Rushdie has been unable to appear in public without multiple bodyguards. He is shown above giving a commencement address at Bard College in New York in 1996.

The British had no intention of sending Rushdie to Iran, so the Iranian government put a bounty on the famous author: An Islamic charitable foundation offered a reward of 20 million *tumans,* which amounted to about one million dollars. The reward has increased several times since then. Khomeini promised anyone willing to go to England to commit the deed "the delights of paradise for eternity" if the assassin was killed in the process. President Khatami, after he was elected in 1997, wanted to bring to a close the *fatwa* on the famous author. At a breakfast, Andrew Rosenthal, the foreign editor of the *New York Times,* asked why Khatami did not lift the death sentence against Rushdie. Khatami, looking annoyed, gave a long-winded answer that left his audience even more confused. It finally emerged, though, that the Rushdie affair was over, at least in Khatami's mind.

Then, in February 1999, more than half the deputies in the Iranian parliament signed a statement declaring, "The verdict on Rushdie, the blasphemer, is death, both today and tomorrow, and to burn in hell for all eternity." The following year, the eleventh year of the *fatwa*, the director of the foundation said that the fatwa was still in place, but it was somewhat encouraging to learn that the organization was bankrupt. Ayatollah Khamenei said in 2005 that it was still in effect, as it can only be rescinded by the man who issued it or a higher authority.

Rushdie spoke about what it was like to always be in fear for your life in an interview with Laura Miller of *Salon.com* in 2006. Miller had to be screened by bodyguards before she could approach him. Rushdie was on tour for the first time in a decade. For a nonsecretive man, the 48-year-old author said, "I've had to keep a lot of secrets." When asked how being afraid affected his writing, he responded, "It never felt like fear, it felt more like disorientation and bewilderment and confusion, and of course these are very bad emotions out of which to write. So it derailed my life for awhile, and I had to climb back onto the rails, I suppose." He said that "the fatwa certainly made me think about [death] a lot more than I ever had." He realized that a lot of his friends had died from AIDS and other diseases and "one doesn't need a fatwa, it can happen anytime." If anyone can understand that statement, it is Shirin Ebadi.

Ali Akbar Hashemi Rafsanjani was elected president in August of that year. After the revolution, he, along with many of his colleagues, confiscated property and money from the Iranians who left the country. He and his family were pistachio farmers, but within 10 years, they ended up owning the country's largest copper mine. The Rafsanjanis took control of the state-owned television network, occupied key positions in the Ministry of Oil, directed the Tehran Metro Construction Project, and ran a company that exports $400 million worth of pistachios annually. He was one among many in the system who had started to live like Hollywood stars. Another was the man who had driven Ayatollah Khomeini from the airport to Tehran when Khomeini had returned to Iran in 1979. Khomeini had appointed the driver, who had been working at a fruit and vegetable stand, as minister of the Revolutionary Guards. Eventually, he gained control of the Mostazafan Foundation, which has assets that exceed $10 million.

Organizations such as Mostazafan foundation exist, it is said, to pay off the mullahs. It is also suspected, according to Gregory Sullivan of the Near Eastern Affairs Bureau at the U.S. State Department, that they provide funding for Iran's shadow foreign policy, which includes sponsorship of Hezbollah, a Lebanese militant organization.[58] Some clerics opposed the corruption, but they had to be careful in voicing their opinion.

After Khomeini's death, the job market for women expanded, and Ebadi received her license to practice law. She set up an office where she dealt with commercial cases. She was amazed at the corruption taking place within the system. There was no justice system in effect, but rather a process where bribes were the effective means of settling disputes. She felt that she was put in the position of "abandoning my principles or failing my clients."[59] She decided to take on pro bono cases, where she could at least put a spotlight on the injustices that were taking place. It was her opinion that the laws needed to go on trial before they could be changed.

As is common with corrupt governments, the economy was in terrible shape, especially for the rural and middle classes. The clerics

Above, Iranian lawmakers, including women wearing traditional garb, listen during a session of parliament in 2004. In the early 1990s, following Ayatollah Khomeini's death, more jobs opened up to the women of Iran.

had to figure out how to maintain the status quo, for they knew the unrest that develops around unemployment and economic stress. They decided to instate new regulations to keep the people in check, and once again they claimed they were interpreting the new laws based on *Sharia,* or Islamic law. Ebadi suspected that the clerics just wanted to keep Iranians cut off from the outside world.

THE PENAL CODE OF 1995

Under the new penal code, adopted in 1995 by the Majlis, or legislative assembly, those found guilty of adultery, witnessed by at least three others, would be subject to execution by stoning. According to a report by the United Nations High Commissioner for Refugees, women caught violating the Islamic dress code could be sentenced to between 10 days and 10 months in prison, or 74 lashes. Some women tried wearing colorful scarves, long coats, and running shoes.[60]

The absolute domination of men in the home was paramount: A man could divorce his wife whenever he wanted and was not required to offer any grounds (reasons). According to Prosecutor General Morteza Mogtadai, "Women were not given the right to instigate divorce because they are prone to emotional and irrational decision-making." A woman was not allowed to leave her home without her husband's permission.

Suicide Among Women in Iran

A disturbing trend developed among women after the revolution. Women were committing suicide in record numbers, in particular by self-immolation, in which the victim burns herself to death. A report in January 1994 listed 3,600 suicides in northeastern Iran; 2,530 of those were women. The reasons given by various groups are many: social humiliation, family insecurity, constant fear for their children, or fear of losing their children, and no safeguards to protect their rights. The conservative newspaper *Kayhan* reported that, in 1994, 880 people had committed suicide in southwestern Iran; of those, 74 percent were women. A story showed up in a women's magazine called *Zan-e-Roux;* in 1994 a 14-year-old high-school girl set herself on fire to evade marrying a 42-year-old man. Another woman who had been constantly harassed by the security forces finally set herself on fire, screaming, "Down with tyranny! Long live freedom! Love live Iran!"

Shirin Ebadi broached the topic in her memoir, *Iran Awakening: A Memoir of Revolution and Hope.* She wrote about a woman who had self-immolated. She was the daughter of a sermon leader. She had tried to divorce her husband, but her father, who was a member of the orthodox clergy, refused to let her. She doused herself with gasoline and lit herself on fire. This was happening with too many women who were educated and yet had nowhere to go; jobs were unavailable, and they could

She was completely at the service of her husband.[61] If a woman died, the sons could take twice as much of the estate as could each daughter.

Women who wanted to leave the country were required to seek written, notarized permission from their husband, father, or legal guardian. Female children could be bought or sold with the consent of a male guardian. They could be forced to marry much older husbands. (This practice continues today, occurring more frequently among the poor, who sell their daughters to buyers in northeast Iran, who put them to work on farms and in workshops. Many commit suicide.)

not tolerate reverting back to the traditional life. Ebadi said, "This tragic exhibitionism [self-immolation], I'm convinced, is women's way of forcing their community to confront the cruelty of their oppression. Otherwise, would it not simply be easier to overdose on pills in a dark room?"*

Donna Hughes, Professor of the Women's Studies Program at the University of Rhode Island, said to a Congressional Breakfast Conference in June 2005:

> In Iran, terror begins at home. The clerics put their ideology into practice in some of the most oppressive and barbaric ways the world has seen in recent times. The first victims were women and girls. . . . Clerics made laws on how to control, punish, torture, and kill women and girls. . . . They perpetually torment and terrorize the female population.

As a result, women and girls in Iran have many health problems related to the abuse. According to Hughes, the suicide rate among girls is among the highest in the world. This is happening, even though it is forbidden by the Koran and considered an act against the will of God.

*Shirin Ebadi, with Azadeh Moaveni, *Iran Awakening: Memoir of Revolution and Hope.* New York: Random House, 2006, p. 109.

Note 1 of article 1210 of the Civil Code states that the age of puberty for a boy is at 15 full lunar years; for a girl, it is 9 full lunar years. A 9-year old girl can be punished as an adult by flogging, execution, and even stoning. Child custody laws tore young children from their mothers if they divorced, and polygamy was acceptable.[62] Torture of women was common, and the methods used were horrible.

ENFORCERS

The morality police, or *Komiteh,* began to prey on everyone, especially women. No one seemed certain just who the Komiteh were. They often arrived on motorcycles carrying knives, chains, and clubs. They had beards and untucked shirts. They were not accountable for their actions. According to Ebadi,

> [they] harassed people because they felt like it, looked for pretexts to intimidate them, and, when they found none, made them up. A bitter look, a misplaced word, the most casual defense of self could provoke them into great rage, and before you knew it, you were three days into an interrogation, being accused of anything from adultery to treason.[63]

According to a report in 1997 by the United Nations Refugee Agency, the Komiteh were not the only ones instructed to enforce Islamic morality. The *Hezbollahi,* the *Pasdaran,* and *Basiji* were groups of religious zealots who also jumped in to enforce Sharia. The Pasdaran was created by Ayatollah Khomeini to maintain internal security. It operated its own intelligence unit, and was also responsible for recruiting and training the Basiji.

A 1993 study by Kenneth Katzman found that the Pasdaran comprised "lower middle class urban guerillas" and later included opportunists looking for "monetary or career gains, as well as conscripts."[64] The Basiji, on the other hand, was made up mainly of teenage boys from rural areas, many of them illiterate and unemployed, who signed up for three-month tours of service. Their job was to support the *Pasdaran* in maintaining security, enforcing Islamic dress and moral codes, promoting Islamic cultural activities, and advising the judiciary.

In her memoir, Ebadi referred to the *lebas shakhsis,* or the plainclothesmen, who were used by the hard-liners to put down unrest. She described them as having stubble, a stocky build, and seedy watchfulness. "They are akin to a local Mafia that terrorizes a neighborhood," she said, "whispering threats in the ears of shop owners, staging violent hits that are designed to instill fear and a permanent sense of insecurity."[65]

WOMEN IN THE 1990S

The population growth rate of Iran was the highest in the world. Since the 1979 revolution, Iran had shifted from being an economically progressive country under the shah to a still-developing country under the ayatollah. Seventy percent of the population lived in absolute poverty, earning less than one dollar a day.[66] The women in particular lived in fear, worrying that an ankle might show or that someone would report them for speaking against the system. The girls, wearing *hejab,* or headscarves, continued to attend segregated schools. Ebadi had to worry constantly about her daughters, making sure that their heads were covered properly and that, at least when in public, they did not make mistakes. She herself was arrested several times for incorrect dress, then released.

Traditional fathers, who previously had kept their daughters at home, slowly began to allow the girls to live in dormitories at the university. Even with the new laws in effect, these girls began to question the authority of their fathers, who, for centuries, had defined their honor through their daughter's virtue. Women were starting to earn more college degrees than men, yet their rate of unemployment remained much higher, and women were not allowed to participate in many fields. Ebadi wrote that these years instilled in women "a visceral consciousness of their oppression."[67]

EBADI STEPS UP

Ebadi felt she was in a perpetual state of frustration. She wrote,

> We lived under an Islamic Republic that was neither going
> anywhere nor inclined to recast its governing ethos as secular;
> the legal system was underpinned by Islamic law; and every
> facet of a woman's place in society—from access to birth con-
> trol to divorce rights to compulsory veiling—was determined
> by interpretations of the Koran.[68]

When she spoke later in an interview in America, she said:

> The Iranian government claims that these laws are Islamic,
> and my job is to prove that these laws are not Islamic but come
> from wrong interpretations of Islamic laws. I have to prove to
> the government that they can change. Islam, like any religion,
> has many interpretations. In Saudia Arabia women cannot
> even drive cars, while in Indonesia and Bangladesh and Paki-
> stan, women can even become prime minister.[69]

It was also true that, in most other Islamic countries, women had
far more judges to turn to who were sympathetic to their requests
for divorce and property rights.

A TRAGIC CASE

In 1996, Ebadi heard of a bizarre case of rape and murder. A
nine-year-old girl, Leila Fathi, was raped in the meadow near
her home by a gang of men, then she was hit on the head and
thrown over a cliff. The three men were caught; one confessed,
then hung himself in jail. The other two denied their part in the
crime, but they were found guilty and sentenced to death. The
family of a victim of homicide or manslaughter had the right to
choose between legal punishment and financial compensation,
referred to as blood money. The judge in the case said that the

Above, Shirin Ebadi is shown lighting the Save the Children peace flame outside of City Hall in Oslo, Norway, in 2003. Throughout her career, Ebadi worked not only to improve conditions for women in Iran, but also for children in her homeland and elsewhere.

girl's family had to come up with thousands of dollars to finance the executions of the two men. Because Iranian law considered a man's life to be worth twice as much as a woman's, hoewever, the "blood money" for the two men was worth more than the life of the murdered child.

Leila's father sold everything he had, including the clay hut where they lived. It was not considered enough. The family slept at the shrine of Ayatollah Khomeini while trying to raise more money. They could not return home because of the shame of Leila's rape. The only way their shame could be erased was by the execution of the rapists. When family members tried to sell their kidneys to raise money, the doctor began to ask questions. He insisted that the judiciary make up the difference from the state treasury, and the chief agreed. Days before the execution, however, one of the men escaped, and the court overruled the verdict of the other.

Ebadi agreed to represent Leila's family, and she presented a simple defense: "It was unjust for a girl to be raped and killed, and for her family to have lost every possession and become homeless through the legal proceedings that followed," she said. "It was unjust that the victims were now being victimized further by the law."[70] Over the following year, both defendants were acquitted, but the verdicts were overturned, and the investigation was reopened. The judge took every opportunity to tell Ebadi that she was speaking against Islam and its sacred laws. The worst thing that could happen was to be called an apostate, or one who challenged Islamic law, and Ebadi knew, in arguing Leila's case, that she was walking a dangerous line. The case was never resolved, but it shone a light on Iranian law with respect to the rights of women and children. The case was written up in newspapers, and the publicity established Ebadi as an advocate for women's and children's rights. Ebadi was learning that the media was a powerful tool.

Women's inferiority in the penal code worried Ebadi, and she realized that few knew what sort of fate awaited them, should they run into similar problems. She wrote a magazine article for *Iran-é Farda,* in which she boldly explained that *diyeh,* which was the section of the penal code that dealt with blood money, equated a man's testicles and a woman's life. Ebadi stated it in her own words, "If a professional woman with a Ph.D. is run over in the street and killed and an illiterate thug gets one of his testicles injured in a fight, the value of her life and his damaged testicle are equal."[71] With that example, she wanted to stress how women were treated as nonpeople. She had no idea the impact such an article would have. The magazine sold out immediately, and a member of parliament expressed fury over it, saying that, if someone did not stop Ebadi, they would have to do it themselves. It was the first time that Ebadi thought the system might fear her. On the other hand, that thought did not lessen her fear of those in power.

CHAPTER 7

Hope Springs Eternal: A Reform Government

I n 1997, it was time to vote for a new president. Rafsanjani could not run again. The clergy criticized his efforts to improve relations with Germany and France, and some even grumbled about their supreme leader, Ali Khamenei, who had replaced Khomeini. He, too, was becoming slightly lenient, taking the middle ground on theological issues. All candidates for public office in both parliamentary and presidential elections had to be approved by the Council of Guardians, so it was unlikely that a popular candidate would be allowed to run.

Seyed Muhammad Khatami had impeccable credentials if taken at face value. He was part of the clerical establishment. He had been a disciple of Ruhollah Khomeini when he was a young boy and was friends with Khomeini's son. His brother married one of Khomeini's granddaughters, and Khatami's wife was a cousin of Khomeini's son. Khatami's sister married a well-known cleric.

Khatami had a checkered career, though. He had been dismissed from his job at the prestigious Kayhan Publishing Company, after which he served as Minister of Islamic Guidance. He was dismissed 10 years later after easing restrictions on films, music, art, and literature. He and the people who worked under

The Islamic Republic's System of Government

Most scholars refer to the government of Iran as a theocracy, a form of government in which officials are considered to be divinely inspired. In an article entitled "Elections and Governmental Structure in Iran: Reform Lurks Under the Flaws," Professor William Beeman of Brown University noted that this system had not been imposed on the Iranian people, and the electoral process remained in place. What had changed, he said, was that "half of the institutions in the Iranian government are unelected, and these institutions have veto power over the elected institutions. Furthermore, the army and the judiciary are controlled by these unelected bodies."*

The structure of the government of the Republic of Iran is as follows: The Grand Ayatollah Khomeini created the role of supreme leader after the 1979 revolution. The Ayatollah Ali Khamenei is the current supreme leader; he was chosen by the clerics who make up the Assembly of Experts. His job is to appoint the director of the judiciary, six of the members of the Guardian Council, the commanders of the armed forces, Friday prayer leaders, and the head of radio and television. The Revolutionary Guard and the regular forces are also under his command.

The Assembly of Experts appoints the supreme leader. Only clerics can be members of the 86 elected members, and the Guardian Council eliminates any candidates they do not want to run. The Guardian Council consists of six clergy appointed by the supreme leader and six jurists nominated by the judiciary and approved by parliament. Council terms last six years. These 12 men have veto power over every electoral candidate, which makes them the most influential political body in Iran. Because of this, they have been accused of rigging elections, although it him encouraged filmmakers to be more open, and his ministers had allowed a progressive newspaper called *Salaam* to operate. New magazines that discussed women's issues appeared on the newsstands. He issued permits for certain books, including some feminist titles. He wrote a book on Western philosophers

is unlikely that they did so in the 2004 election, as the percentage figures in favor of current rulers was not that high.

The president is elected for four years and can only serve two terms. He is head of the executive branch of government, and his job is to make sure the constitution is followed. His powers are limited, as the clerics who fill most of the unelected positions and the supreme leader have power over him. The Iranian presidential cabinet is called the Council of Ministers; members are chosen by the president and approved by parliament. They are watched closely by the clergy, to make sure they follow Sharia, or strict Islamic codes of conduct.

The members of the judiciary are responsible for making certain that the Islamic laws are enforced, and they help to define legal policy. They nominate the six lay members of the Guardian Council, and the director reports to the supreme leader. The Expediency Council is an advisory body; the Supreme Leader appoints its members. If the representatives in the Majlis, or legislative assembly, refuse to do what the Guardian Council dictates—for example, change a law with which the Council disagrees—then the Expediency Council will ensure that it happens.

There are 296 members of the Majlis, who are elected every four years. Members can introduce and pass bills, but all have to be approved of by the Guardian Council, who are always conservative. Members of the Council of Ministers are the president's cabinet, and he is allowed to choose them, but every move they make is watched by the supreme leader.

*Beeman, William O., "Elections and Governmental Structures in Iran: Reform Lurks Under the Flaws." *Brown Journal of World Affairs*, Summer/Fall 2004. Volume XI, Issue 1, p. 1.

and another book entitled *Fear of Waves,* in which he stated that "Islam was no longer responsive to modern life, especially when it came to freedom."[72]

The country was in poverty, although with 9 percent of the world's oil and 15 percent of its natural gas, it should by all rights have been one of the wealthiest. The per capita income was lower than what it was before the revolution. The citizens of Iran were looking for change. Just prior to the 1997 election, the conservatives put up a bland candidate, and then issued tirades against Khatami. What they failed to realize was that millions of women wanted equality and respect. Khatami said that he would make elected institutions answerable to the people. To the consternation of the clerics and conservatives, he was elected. He told CNN that "Iran's reformists sought what the Puritans had sought when they landed in America—Freedom and God."[73]

Khatami was basically an unknown, yet 22 million Iranians went to the polls to vote for the man who spoke of creating an Islamic democracy. It was the first time in many years that the race felt at least slightly competitive. Ebadi recalled later that, on Election Day, she did not see one woman wearing a chador, and it was the first time her mother, who was 80 years old, had voted since the 1979 revolution.[74]

Iranians were curious about the bookish man who wore elegant robes and fine leather loafers. His election was a statement about what they did not want: the corrupt clerics and all their hypocrisy. At the time of the revolution, there were about 80,000 clerics in Iran; 20 years later the count was 600,000 or more. Most Iranians were working two jobs just to pay their bills. Khatami emerged separate from all the dogmatism that the Iranians were weary of hearing, as well as the "death to America" slogans, which were also tired. He spoke English, German, and Arabic, in addition to Persian, and he focused on young people and women, often referring to their importance in society.

The main danger was that people wanted change, and they wanted it fast, but they forgot that the president of the Islamic

Seyed Muhammad Khatami, shown above in a portrait from 1997, was elected the president of Iran that year. Though virtually unknown before his campaign for the presidency, Khatami won the race on his promise to create an Islamic democracy.

Republic of Iran has little actual power. Once in office, Khatami worked within the system, but he also talked about creating a civil society that reconciled the sacred and the secular. He called for the rule of law and extended individual rights and basic freedoms. Ayatollah Khamenei and Khatami were peers, and their families knew each other. Khamenei had stepped in when the revered Ayatollah Khomeini died, but he never felt he was qualified to lead.

It was the differences of the two men rather than the similarities that stood out to their public. Khatami wanted to heal the rift between Iran and the United States, but Khamenei continued to condemn the country that clerics liked to blame for all of Iran's problems. Khatami told CNN News in 1998 that he wanted to break down the wall of mistrust with the United States through cultural exchanges. Khatami and Khamenei needed each other— one had power on paper, the other had the support of the people. Elaine Sciolino wrote that Khatami's focus on tolerance was part of his undoing. She said, "He believed that transparency in the political system was the key to curbing corruption and promoting economic growth."[75] If he could create a society governed by the rule of law, the country would prosper.

Although the Islamic regime in those years still did not tolerate criticism, there had been a slight mellowing, at least in public, of the brutal reactions of the authorities. That was the impression, at least. The truth was much darker, however. Repression and terror had come and gone in waves for many years, but in 1998, the people relaxed their guard a little. A theologian published a book in which he analyzed the 10 sayings attributed to the Prophet and the imams, which had been presented since the beginning of the revolution as the reason why clerical rule was necessary. He said that 8 of these were probably not authentic. Even the remaining 2 could not be used to justify the political power the clerics had. He saw no justification for the absolute guardianship of the appointed jurist, or the supreme leader.[76]

REIGN OF TERROR

Suddenly, a reign of terror spread; the first victims were Dariush and Parveneh Forouhar, who were brutally murdered in their home by people they knew. Thousands attended their funeral. The killings continued and caused many writers to sleep in different houses each night, in an attempt to avoid a surprise attack. By the time the onslaught was over, 80 writers and activitsts had disappeared.[77] The conservatives were not prepared for the boldness of the new progressive newspapers, which demanded answers. The government tried to placate the people by expressing their innocence, but the people did not back down. A shake-up occurred in the Ministry of Intelligence and Security as a result, and the minister resigned. The conservatives hoped that such an action would show that they were earnest in their attempts to find the truth.

A 39-year-old columnist named Akbar Ganji, who wrote for the progressive newspaper called *This Morning*, named several people who had been murdered during Rafsanjani's reign.[78] He had gone within the Iranian intelligence organization to find the secret state plan to eliminate critics of the government. He discovered that senior clerics had issued the fatwas, or Islamic decrees that served as death sentences. He wrote articles about his findings, and the Iranian people rushed out to read them. Parliament began to consider a restrictive press law after shutting down *Salaam*.

Once again, life was nerve-wracking for Ebadi, who now had teenagers at home who questioned everything. She felt it was her job to teach them to walk the delicate line between obedience and protest, a challenging prospect, as they were young and felt invincible, and they had watched their mother fight the system most of their lives.

UNIVERSITY A HOTBED

The population in Tehran at that time—12 million—was described by writer Elaine Sciolino as comparable to having 50 million people in New York City.[79] The city was overwhelmed by masses of people who had responded to Khomeini's call for them to have more children. Women volunteers went door to door to discuss birth control. The university was a breeding ground for unrest and impatience. When students heard about the magazine *Salaam* being forced to close, they protested. The government's reaction was immediate and brutal. Paramilitaries in plain clothes entered university grounds, threw students off balconies, and beat and shot them. One student was killed, and 300 were hospitalized. The unrest spread to the provinces. Rioting started. With its smashed storefronts and gutted-out buildings, Tehran looked like a civil war zone.

Shirin Ebadi took the opportunity to show her daughters the dangers that lurked outside. They passed parents wailing outside the notorious Evin Prison, hoping to hear if their children had been arrested. She did her best to impress upon her children the dangers of falling into traps, where they could become pawns of infiltrators trying to get students arrested. They had to be reminded that, if they were caught, they would be treated worse than anyone. Negar disobeyed her mother the next day and went to the university campus with her friends. Hearing gunshots, they ran to a house across the street, where they had a better view of the rioting. Ebadi tried to call the house, but there was no answer. When the streets were less chaotic, Ebadi rescued her daughter. She lectured Negar about her actions, which could have such grave consequences in Tehran.[80]

The rioting continued for six days before President Khatami stepped forward. He told the students that they were attacking the foundations of the regime and wanting to create tensions and disorders. He gave them a severe warning. The students were stunned. It was true that groups of young people had started shouting "death to the supreme leader," but the students insisted that these people had been sent in by the hardliners, which was probably the truth.

Ebadi wrote in her memoir, "That summer was a turning point for the motley assortment of religious nationalists, secularists, former regime loyalists, and intellectuals loosely known as the reform movement."[81] With the groups splintering off from each other, the dream of a reformist movement was over.

A HEAVY CASELOAD

Ebadi was nearing 50, and she found herself torn between her cases, writing, and doing all the domestic chores; she was too conditioned to change. With her overwhelming workload, she felt that she was away from home too much, so she tried to balance her absences by bringing her work home. She felt more compelled than ever to take on cases that involved human rights issues.

One case revolved around a child named Arian, who had been forced to live with her abusive father after her mother divorced him. Weighing 33 pounds at death, the nine-year-old had been battered to death and burned with cigarettes. Ebadi had long been concerned with the laws regarding child custody, thinking the current laws were the most destructive of all the legal codes. It simply was not right that a mother had no rights in the case of divorce and that children were automatically handed over to their fathers. Ebadi wanted attention brought to the case.

Ebadi and some colleagues arranged a ceremony to mourn the child's death, reserving space in a large mosque. Ebadi's husband's uncle, a cleric, told the story of Arian's short and brutal life. At the service, another man lifted a boy up in the air and charged the people to do something for children like him, who wanted to be with his mother. Ebadi went to the microphone in the women's section and announced that it was time to reform the law. Child laws and women's custody rights were suddenly a hot topic. Ebadi's phone did not stop ringing with people wanting her help.

At the trial for Arian's death, Ebadi put the law on trial, along with the criminal. The judge subtly accused her of defaming religion, and she begged to disagree. She explained that she was criticizing a law that had been passed by the Iranian parliament.

The stepbrother, who had actually killed her, was sentenced to death, and the father and stepmother to a year in prison. In an act of compassion, the mother stayed the stepbrother's execution. The stepbrother was a child of the father's second marriage, and he had also been taken from his mother and abused. Something subtle was happening: The Islamic government began to realize that, because of worldwide attention on their actions, they would have to be more careful about human rights abuses in their country.

During 1999 and 2000, Ganji was the most controversial man in Iran. It was not just because he had shed light on all of the murders; he was also relentless in his demands for an explanation. The fame that accompanied his articles and interviews was his only protection. He acted as if he did not fear death, and his colleagues revered him. It was the Golden Age of Iranian journalism,[82] and writers were using every opportunity, aware that their freedom could end at any moment.

In his writing, Ganji used metaphors and aliases that his readers would understand. Journalist Christopher de Bellaigue wrote about Ganji, "He got his public used to an allegation of astonishing impudence, without making that allegation explicit."[83] Ganji led his enthralled readers to higher and higher leaders in their government, again, without naming names, until he reached President Rafsanjani, debatably the most powerful and the richest man in Iran. Rafsanjani, who had called his reign the cleanest in the history of the Intelligence Ministry, was facing a sullied reputation.

At the end of 2000, Ganji was tried for taking part in a conference in Berlin. He was cocky in the courtroom, and at the end of the trial he announced that the state was trying to blackmail him for his investigations into the serial killings. He was sentenced to 15 years, 10 years in prison and 5 in exile. In the elections that year, Rafsanjani did not win a seat, and retaliation was in order. Thirty reformist newspapers were banned, and more than a dozen journalists were jailed. In 2001, three Intelligence Ministry agents were sentenced to death, and two boys were sentenced to life imprisonment. The real criminals remained safe behind their titles. Some of the reformists were unhappy with Ganji for pushing things too far, but many others considered him a hero.

At the time, Ebadi participated in her own trials, either defending victims of the system or defending herself. She had not lost sight of Ganji, however. While he served time in prison, he wrote a book entitled *A Manifesto for Republicanism,* in which he called for a full separation between religion and the state. He called on the supreme leader to step down. It was the first time that someone had called for the Islamic system to be replaced by a secular democracy. He encouraged those who wanted democracy to fight for it, to create civil disobedience. Ebadi ran into him one day in prison, and he told her that the court had agreed to reduce his sentence if he chose a certain lawyer, but of course they would not keep that promise. Ebadi offered to take on his case, but in the end she realized that the authorities would never allow her to get close to him.

Ebadi's world was filled with one trial after another. Her book *History and Documentation of Human Rights in Iran* was published in 2000. The preface states, "This small work represents a genuine effort on the part of the author to clarify the legal aspects of human rights and the instances of the violation of such rights in various legal enactments."[84] Through her trial work, she attempted to shame the members of the Islamic regime into changing some of the laws that kept her people oppressed. It could not have been a more dangerous undertaking. Shirin Ebadi had long ago learned to live with fear, however. She wrote in her memoir, "And so I remind myself that the greatest threat of all is my own fear; that it is our fear, the fear of Iranians who want a different future, that makes our opponents powerful."[85]

CHAPTER 8

From Jail to Nobel Peace Prize

During the student riots, Ezzat Ebrahimnezhad was killed by the *lebas shakhsis*, the thugs who operated under the orders of the hardliners. After reading that Ebrahimnezhad's father was willing to sell his house to hire a lawyer to pursue his son's murderers, Ebadi got in touch with him and offered her services for free. A bogus trial had been held by the Tehran police chief and his officers, and in the end, one charge was filed against an officer for stealing an electric shaver from a dorm room.

Undeterred, Ebadi continued with the case, and eventually a young female student came forth as a witness to the crime. The justice system played games as usual, passing the case around to various departments, where it would sit until someone would declare it out of their jurisdiction. Ebadi set out to find evidence, however, and in March 2000, a young man appeared in her office. He said that he had been a member of the lebas shakhsis and that he had information about his comrades who had killed Ebrahimnezhad. His name was Amir Farshad Ebrahimi, and he claimed that, because he wanted to get out, the others were trying to frame him. He said that they had jailed and tortured him. Ebadi's advice for him was to go public. "It's safer for you that way," she said. "Your secrets are dangerous to you as secrets, but once they are out in the public realm, it's over."[86]

Ebadi knew her phones were tapped, so she planned all the details for taping Ebrahimi, even asking two people to join them as witnesses. When Ebrahimi showed up, his sister was with him, and Ebadi was surprised to see her wearing makeup and painted nails. Ebadi led them to a room, where she began to film his testimony. During the process, an American human rights worker called Ebadi into the other room and said she thought it had to be a trap. She was worried that they would arrest Ebadi for falsifying information against the Islamic Republic.

Ebadi was simply gathering information for her case, which was not an illegal act. She, too, was beginning to have second thoughts. The following day, she turned the tape over to the deputy interior minister. To her horror, the newspapers began to print stories about a tape that exposed the actions of the notorious group *Ansar-e-Hezbollah* (not related to the Lebanese military group). Ebadi learned that Ebrahimi's mother was interviewed and she claimed that her son had been brainwashed into making the tape. It did not help that Ebrahimi had disappeared. The hard-line papers were filled with attacks on people who were negative about the revolution. To have one's name show up in print on the front page meant that an arrest would follow. Sure enough, Ebadi was called in for an interrogation, which filled her with anxiety. She wrote a letter to her family telling them she was going to prison, but assuring them that she would be fine.

The call came as expected. She would be going to Evin Prison, where practically every political prisoner in the past 50 years had been taken. It was where her brother-in-law had died, along with many others. Her husband, Javad, took her to court in the evening, and, within 20 minutes, she was sentenced and led out a back door. When she arrived at the prison, she was asked if she had been brought in for a moral offense. The question amused her, for she was being asked if she was a prostitute. She laughed hysterically, which did not go over well with the guards. The cell she was taken to was filthy, and there was no running water in the sink. A dirty, rusted toilet was in the corner. The guard left, and Ebadi was alone in prison. She wrote later, "I had no recourse to anyone or anything, except God."[87]

All the guards had college degrees, and they knew about the children's rights organization that Ebadi had helped to found, so they were respectful of her. Most of the prisoners were drug addicts who had been incarcerated without any detoxification drugs. They screamed through the night. On the third night, she was rudely awakened by a female guard, who announced that Ebadi was being moved to another prison. Ebadi was overcome with fear. They refused to answer her questions about where she was being taken. She was blindfolded and put on a bus.

When Ebadi got off the bus, she recognized the voice of Ali, the man who had interrogated her in court. He told her they were convening a court session for her. Rage replaced the fear when she realized the injustice of her situation, and she began to scream at Ali. He had her take off the blindfold and told her that she was in a place with better water and food. He promised her that she would be more comfortable. The next day, an abusive woman guard kicked her awake and threw a dirty chador at her to wear. When the doctor came, she was allowed to have her own clothes back. The new prison was exceedingly lonely and silent. Four resentful women guards were around, but she was not allowed a radio or newspapers. The lights were always on, and there were no windows, which she found disorienting. There were hours of interrogation. She prayed five times a day, and tried to do calisthenics.

After another week, she was put on a minibus to the courthouse. Amir Farshad Ebrahimi was there, dressed in a prison uniform. Well-wishers and journalists lined the way. Ebrahimi stuck to his original testimony, but Ebadi knew he would be tortured to change it. Ebadi's husband was there with an attorney who would represent her. Across the room, Ebadi's eyes interlocked with her sister's. That was all the contact Ebadi had with her family.

Another week passed, and Ebadi began to hallucinate. She had never been more uncomfortable. She finally picked up a spoon and tried to carve into the wall: "We are born to suffer because we are born in the Third World. Space and time are imposed on us. There is nothing to do but stay patient."[88]

Another trial took place, and Ebadi's husband was able to speak on his wife's behalf. She refused to have her daughters see her. Much to her surprise, she was called to the phone and a judge told her that she could be released if she paid the equivalent of $25,000. It had been 25 days since she had entered the prison. She called her husband and asked him to come to get her and to bring the deed to their house. She stopped the taxi on the way home to pick up newspapers; when she arrived, her relatives were gathered outside. Her daughters ran to her. That evening family and friends collected in the living room and drank tea together. Ebadi, dealing with some of the worst crimes imaginable, was already in the habit of protecting her girls, and this was no different. She simply behaved as though she had been away at a conference. The girls presented her with a folder of messages from all over the world, and she realized that she had acquired an international reputation. As for the murder of Ezzat Ebrahimnezhad, the judge dismissed the case. All the student protestors felt abandoned, both by the reformists and by their president.

CAUTIOUS CHANGE

Although the student revolt had awful results, and 88 intellectuals had been assassinated, from 1997 to 2005, there was less interference in people's lives. The morality police, while still active, were looked on more as nuisances than anything else. In 2000, the reformists swept the parliament, and 14 progressive female members of parliament (MPs) entered the legislature. The ratio was similar to female representatives in European countries. Incredibly, they were never given anywhere to sit. When Ebadi went to the private women's chamber to draft a resolution on family law, she was shocked to see an empty room with a rug on the floor. The female MPs preferred the empty room to the room where the men were located, because they could remove their chadors.

Ebadi's girls wore brightly colored scarves and sometimes left the house with no socks. With the new, more relaxed atmosphere, cafés and galleries opened, and outdoor concerts were held in parks. The Internet opened up a new world to the young. Hundreds of thousands of college graduates were being churned out, but the job market was competitive, and there was no real chance for advancement. The young started moving to other countries, which caused another brain drain.

Although there was more tolerance, Ebadi always had to be on guard. The journalist Ganji attended a conference in Berlin, Germany, in 2000. When he returned, he was accused of being "anti-Islamic" and sentenced to 10 years in prison. The conviction was eventually appealed, but in the end he was sent to prison for 6 years on charges of collecting papers harmful to national security. That same year, he was given the International Press Freedom Award by Canadian Journalists for Free Expression.

The ayatollahs were growing sick of the reformist newspapers. In 2001, Ebadi was warned to drop a case involving a journalist friend. One evening when she was returning home with her two daughters, a man approached them and said that he needed legal assistance. She told him to come to her office, but when a wedding party started toward them, he ran off. She was certain he was an assassin. When she told a friend by phone, she was later threatened for spreading false rumors about an imaginary assassin. That year she also created the Defenders of Human Rights Center to bring lawyers together to work pro bono for dissidents. She served as its president.

The day arrived in 2003 when Ebadi and her husband had to sit down with their daughter Negar to decide her future. In the end, they decided that she should go to Montreal to attend graduate school. Ebadi was filled with sadness the day her daughter left. She whispered to her, "I just hope that after you finish, you'll come back. . . . I just want you to be certain of one thing. I know it's not easy here . . . but know that your heart will be more comfortable in a country that is your own."[89]

Then, in June 2003, students at East Tehran University started another protest after some of their peers were injured in a protest held earlier that day. They called for President Khatami to resign. The word spread, and students at other universities joined in. Students began calling for the end of the Islamic system. They had backpacks full of rocks and were screaming for change. There was anger and despair in their cries. It went on for six evenings, until the authorities sent in their security forces. Police vehicles and trucks filled with soldiers moved through the streets. American President George Bush had praised the protests, which only incensed the Iranian government, causing them to crack down harder on the students. In the end, 4,000 students were missing, and parents once again began to line up at Evin Prison in the hope of securing their release.

Young Iranian-Canadian photographer Zahra Kazemi began to take pictures of the prison. A guard spotted her and demanded that she turn over her camera. She exposed the film while showing him her press card. They argued, and Kazemi told him that he could have the camera, but the film was hers. She was held at the prison and interrogated. Four days later, she was sent to a hospital in a coma. A week later she died.

The government of Canada demanded that her body be sent to Montreal, and they wanted her killers punished. Though excuses were offered, an Iranian vice president finally said that she had been beaten to death. The world was up in arms. Prison officials had called her mother, who was in the city of Shiraz, to come to see her daughter. When she arrived, they told her that her daughter was sick and had been hospitalized. When the mother entered the room and checked under her daughter's nightgown, she said that "her breasts, her arms, the insides of her thighs were all scratched up, and mottled with angry, blue-gray bruises."[90]

Kazemi's mother wanted to send her daughter's body back to Canada, but the authorities insisted that she be buried in Iran. They tricked her mother into signing papers to settle on the case, and she went to Ebadi, who took on the case. Ebadi stayed in the background until the court decided whether or not to have a closed trial; if they knew she was involved, there would be no question. Kazemi's mother wrote a letter saying that her lawyer was God. International attention was focused on the trial, and Ebadi knew it was her chance to bring attention to the prison atrocities. In the end, the judge said that it was impossible to identify which guard had abused Kazemi.

History of the Nobel Peace Prize

Alfred Nobel died on December 10, 1896. The year before, he had written a will stating that he wanted most of his vast wealth to be used for five prizes, including one for peace. The prize for peace was to be awarded to that person who "shall have done the most or the best work for fraternity between nations, for the abolition or reduction of standing armies and for the holding of peace congresses." His dear friend Bertha von Suttner, who published the antiwar novel *Lay Down Your Arms,* was believed to have been influential in his desire to create a peace prize. It is curious that the peace prize was to be awarded by a Norwegian committee while the other four were to be handled by Swedish committees. Opinions vary about the reason for that. Norway was in union with Sweden, and Nobel's will was written in Paris at the Swedish-Norwegian Club. Did Nobel think of Norway as being a more peace-oriented and more democratic country than Sweden? Was he cognizant of the Norwegian Storting's (parliament) interest in the peaceful solutions of international disputes? It is known that he was a fan of writer and peace activist Bjornstjerne Bjornson. Did this influence him?

It took three years before the first prize was awarded, to Frederic Passy and Jean Henry Dunant. Passy was one of the primary founders of the Inter-Parliamentary Union and the main

THE NOBEL PEACE PRIZE

Shirin Ebadi was extremely unpopular with the government of Iran's Islamic regime at this point. She was invited to attend a seminar on Tehran in Paris. The Iranian embassy protested that she did not carry the same beliefs as the Iranian government and should not attend, but the officials in Paris were adamant. It was September, and Ebadi and her younger daughter, Nargess, took in the sights of Paris. On their last night, they stayed with the vice president of the International Federation of Human Rights Leagues.

On the morning they were to leave for Tehran, Ebadi received a phone call. A man on the other end of the phone said he was

organizer of the first Universal Peace Conference. He was the leader of the French peace movement as well. Dunant founded the International Red Cross in 1863. Thus a broad definition of peace was established early on. In 1905, Nobel's old friend von Suttner was awarded the prize, the first woman to receive it. During the years of the First World War (1914–1918), no prize was awarded.

The years from 1919 to 1939 were irregular years, when either no prize was given or it came late. Some of that was due to internal tensions, and members who would not bend. Again, during World War II (1939–1945) no prizes were given. Norway joined the United Nations in 1945, and many of the prizes after that were related to that organization. The peace prize in the years between the late 1940s and 1966 focused on people who worked for human rights, which was the fastest growing field of interest for the committee. In the 1970s and 1980s, laureates hailed from Africa, Asia, and Latin America, as well as North America and Western Europe. By the 1970s, all continents except Australia and Oceania were represented. Shirin Ebadi was the tenth woman to be awarded the Nobel Peace Prize.*

_____

*Geir Lundestad, *The Nobel Peace Prize 1901–2000.* March 15, 2001.

Shirin Ebadi is pictured above wearing a veil during an interview on December 4, 2003, six days before she officially received the Nobel Peace Prize. At that time, Ebadi told the press that she would cast off her headscarf when she traveled to Oslo to formally accept the prize.

calling from the Nobel Peace Prize Committee and asked her to remain where she was. Ebadi thought it was a prank and put the phone down. The phone rang again. She picked it up and was told the same thing. She said that she had to get to the airport, so the caller passed the phone to another voice, who said that Ebadi was a candidate for the prize and should wait. Someone in the background said that she had won the prize, and Ebadi sat down, wondering what to do next.

Journalists began to call. She called a friend, unsure about what to do. He advised her to postpone her flight, because the Iranian government might not be pleased. He told her that he would arrange a press conference. A representative from the Iranian

Embassy arrived and told her that the ambassador sent his congratulations. Later, when they realized that she would not make accusations against them in public, they sent a gift of the Koran to her. Everything was a whirlwind as she decided to return to Tehran the following day.

When she and her daughter boarded the plane, the captain came to congratulate her and moved them up to first class. He told her that he would call this trip the Flight of Peace. On her homeward flight, Ebadi's mind was racing:

> Our struggling NGO could finally have office furniture (The Nobel Peace Prize that year was $1.3 million American.) . . . . What would the Iranian government think? . . . Or would it aggravate those in Iran whose tolerance for me was already limited, who had planned to have me killed when I was infinitely less prominent?[91]

CHAPTER 9

A Memoir and More Threats

badi's memoir, written with Azadeh Moaveni, was entitled *Iran Awakening: A Memoir of Revolution and Hope.* It was published in the United States in May 2006, to rave reviews in American magazines such as *More* and *Ms.* it was also excerpted in many publications, including the *New York Times Magazine.* Ironically, at the same time, the current Iranian president, Mahmoud Ahmadinejad, and President George Bush were in a public dispute over Iran's right to nuclear power. The Iranian government claimed it would be used for electricity, and Bush was convinced that the Iranians were making nuclear weapons. The controversy sparked concerns among Americans after the debacle in Iraq, and for Iranians who, after revolution and an eight-year war with Iraq, were completely opposed to any more confrontation.

Ebadi pointed out in speeches she gave all around America that, for the moment, there were more comparisons to be made between the two countries than there are contrasts. She said in an interview, "What Mr. Bush says is very much like what Mr. Ahmadinejad says. For example, when Mr. Bush says he has a mission from God to settle the problems in the Middle East, Mr. Bush sometimes wants to bring democracy through the use of force, like the government of Iran wants to push people by force into paradise."[92]

Ebadi makes many such comparisons, but she is not alone in doing so. Kenneth Pollack, author of *The Persian Puzzle,* and formerly of the CIA and a member of the National Security Council, has stated that, if the two countries could remove all the historical baggage, it would be hard to figure out why they were in conflict.[93]

The events of July 2006 bring the ongoing conflicts into perspective, however. Members of Hezbollah, a southern Lebanese militia organization with Iranian ties, kidnapped Israeli soldiers, which ignited a new international crisis. Once again, the governments of the United States and Iran were verbally sparring in the media, though there was no public conversation between the two presidents. Ebadi can laugh over the fact that in Iran she is too much of a reformer for her life in Iran to be comfortable, yet on the other hand she is too committed to peaceful change and working within the system to be fully understood outside her own country.

In her memoir, Ebadi said,

> I focus on the political process not because I imagine we will refashion a new relationship around the negotiating table anytime soon but because I see no other options ahead. Iran, for its part, must peacefully transition to a democratic government that represents the will of the majority.

That majority is the young and women. She added,

> For in the end, the Iranian Revolution has produced its own opposition, not least a nation of educated, conscious women who are agitating for their rights. They must be given the chance to fight their own fights, to transform their country interrupted.[94]

(continues on page 90)

Shirin Ebadi Versus the United States

Ebadi, when she began to think about writing her memoir, turned to the United States because she knew that in Iran it would be banned or censored. Americans have the First Amendment, which protects literary and artistic expression from official censorship. She assumed that a country that had freedom of speech would provide her with the opportunity to share her thoughts.

An outmoded and discriminatory United States Treasury Department regulation in effect, however, kept her from doing that. The Office of Foreign Assets Control (OFAC) prohibited the translation, editing, promotion, or marketing of any work from an embargoed state unless the work had been previously published in the writer's home country. They referred Ebadi to a 1917 law that "allows the president to bar transactions during times of war or national emergency." The law was amended to exempt publishers, but the Treasury Department ruled it "illegal to enhance the value of anything created in Iran without permission." This included books.

Ebadi said in an interview with New American Media reporter Brian Shott, in May 2006 that

> I was told that because the U.S has economic sanctions against Iran, I could not publish my books, because proceeds would go to me, and thus to Iran since I live there. I argued that cultural exchanges should be excluded from economic sanctions, and that by refusing to publish my book here, you are actually imposing censorship on the American people.*

Ebadi's agent, Wendy Strothman, said, "If you lift a pencil to help her shape her manuscript so American audiences can read it, you are subject to punishment." The price? Ten years in prison and a fine of $250,000 for an individual or one million dollars for a publishing house.

Basically, publication of Ebadi's memoir was banned in America. Reza Aslan of *The Nation* wrote,

> They were in effect censoring a liberal Muslim reformer who has spent her entire life battling the very Islamic extremists that the United States is so keen to defeat.

Eventually, agency personnel suggested that she apply for a license. Ebadi, however, was in no mood for compromise. She and her agent initiated a lawsuit against the Treasury Department in federal court. Other groups, like the PEN American Center, joined in. They claimed that the OFAC law was unconstitutional. Shirin Ebadi asked, "What is the difference between the censorship in Iran and this censorship in the United States?"** American writers were also chafing over U.S. government discouragement of the publication of dissident speech from oppressive regimes. In December 2004, Ellen Goodman of the *Washington Post* wrote a column titled "Will Her Voice Ever Be Heard?" about Ebadi's situation. In it, she said that the rule bans writers in Sudan, Cuba, and North Korea, adding, "Some are authors of such aid-the-enemy books as *The Field Guide to the Birds of Cuba*."

At the end of 2004, the Treasury Department, with new leadership, lifted most of the restrictions on the publication of foreign writing. Ebadi's book was published in 2006.

---

*Shott, Brian, "Iran Awakening—An Interview with Shirin Ebadi." New America Media. Available at http://news.newamericamedia.org/news/view_article.html.

**Aslan, Reza, "Woman Warrior," *The Nation,* May 29, 2006. Available at http://www.thenation.com/doc/20060529/aslan.

(continued from page 87)

Tara, a woman who was recorded for a book entitled *Voices From Iran: The Changing Lives of Iranian Women* (the author, Mahnaz Kousha, used only first names to identify the interviewees), said,

> Women are a tremendous source of power, but their potential hardly is used in this country. . . . The Revolution brought to the surface women's issues. Women and their concerns have gained tremendous significance. It is like a flood. . . . Nothing can stop this tide. . . . There are and will be victims for sure . . . but women have started to demand their rights and they will get them.[95]

In June 2006, hundreds of Iranian women were beaten and detained for demonstrating for women's rights. As this book goes to press, Ebadi is representing them.

Eight million citizens of Iran were born after the 1979 revolution. The cleric system is no longer effective, and the young are seeking reform. Azadeh Moaveni, author of *Lipstick Jihad: A Memoir of Growing Up Iranian in America and American in Iran,* said, "Iranian young people want secular government, and they want reform, but they know they have to work from within."[96]

THE MKO TODAY

Recent reports indicate that the U.S. Pentagon has been using the Mojahedin-e Khalgh Organization (MKO) to conduct stealth operations in Iran from bases in Iraq and Pakistan, which has sent the clerical regime into a panic.[97] A 2003 headline from the Pacific News Service read, "Paris Raid Reveals Washington's Fractured Iran Policy." Professor William Beeman pointed out that it was clear that the United States was hopeful that the MKO would be the one to create regime change in Iran. Members of that organization, after being ousted from Iran, went to France, Norway, and finally to the United States. Later, the group was established in Iraq.

Above, Shirin Ebadi is pictured with the chairman of the Norwegian Nobel Committee at the ceremony where she received the Nobel Peace Prize. She holds the official diploma associated with the prize, and he holds the accompanying medal.

The U.S. State Department and some members of Congress dislike the organization, and in 1997, the State Department declared the MKO a terrorist organization. They are liked by the Defense Department and other members of Congress, however. It is a controversial subject today. Beeman is deeply suspicious of Alireza Jafarzadeh, a spokesperson for the MKO who works as an independent analyst for Fox News. It was he, according to Beeman, who claimed that Iran has nuclear capabilities. "In fact," Beeman said, "According to the International Atomic Energy Association and its director Mohamed Elbaradei, there is no evidence that Iran is pursuing nuclear weapons."[98]

President Mahmoud Ahmadinejad is a political wild card, meaning no one knows what he will do or how far he will go. Laura Secor, when interviewed for the *New Yorker,* said,

> Perhaps Ahmadinejad won't roll back the reformists' gains in social and political freedom-he'll just freeze the situation as it is. Or maybe he'll clamp down on political freedoms. . . .

Critics of the Peacemaker

The hardliners continue to harass the most famous Iranian woman, but they also do not want to stir up a storm of international criticism. A firsthand account of Ebadi receiving the Nobel Peace Prize was reported by Nasrin Alavi in her book, *We Are Iran: The Persian Blogs,* "Naturally, she [Ebadi] is disdained by the clerics and Iran's state-controlled media ignored the story of her winning the Nobel Peace Prize for many hours. Eventually, there was a brief 15-second announcement at the end of the late evening news, though it omitted any mention of her human rights work, stating merely that she had been awarded the peace prize for her work with 'a children's charity.'" A BBCNews headline read "Peace award divides Iran" in October of 2003. In the article, Jim Muir wrote, "While her [Ebadi's] supporters in the reform movement were clearly delighted, hardliners who don't share her liberal views were not pleased to see the outside world honouring someone they regard as a dissident." Amir Mohebian, who is a commentator at the hardline newspaper *Resalat,* was quoted as saying, "This prize carried the message that Europe intends to put further pressure on human rights issues in Iran as a political move to achieve its particular objectives."*

The final possibility, which isn't incompatible with the first two, is that even if Ahmadinejad tries to roll back the reforms, Khamenei, who is more pragmatic, will stop him."[99]

In May 2006, Ahmadinejad sent an 18-page letter to President Bush, proposing new ways to end the dispute over Iran's development of nuclear technology. President Bush called it a publicity stunt. In August 2006, Ahmadinejad was interviewed by Mike Wallace on the popular American news program *60 Minutes.* The two men argued their points about Hezbollah, Israel, and many other issues. The interview ultimately proved to be confusing, however.

Some influential Iranian-Americans who favor a more aggressive policy toward Iran felt frustration. In the wake of the recent presidential election of Mahmoud Ahmadinejad and the consolidation of the conservatives' control over every level of government, they feel that the days when the clerical system could be reformed from within have come and gone. For them, the only option left is to destroy the regime by any means necessary and build a new Iran from its ashes. Some go so far as to say that Ebadi has betrayed Iranians by not speaking out more about the human rights abuses in Iran. Some, however, might resent her independence of thought and her refusal to join any ideological camps.

Scott Peterson, writing for the *Christian Science Monitor,* said that "for some devout Muslims, she is perceived as a faithless betrayer of Islam, a 'Western Mercenary' and an embarrassment to Iran." Members of the MKO, of which her brother-in-law was a member before he was assassinated, would like her to be more keen on unseating the current regime, but she is much more focused on creating democratic reform in a peaceful manner.

---

*Available at http://newsvote.bbc.co.uk/mpapps/pagetools/print/news.bbc.co.uk/l/hi/world/middle_east/3.

THE INTERNET

When asked in an interview with Matt Dellinger about people in Iran writing articles for the Internet, Laura Secor said,

> It's really important. There are tens of thousands of blogs in Iran. Most of them aren't political in the conventional sense, but writing frankly about private life in Iran is necessarily political, and many of the bloggers do that. The regime is scrambling to censor the Internet, but they can't quite keep up.[100]

The majority of them are people writing frankly about private life in Iran. Authorities are using filtering technology and manage to block a lot of Web sites, but many bloggers have managed to bypass that.

The population of Iran has access to computers, satellite dishes, and all forms of information technology. On August 14, 2006, the BBC News Web site published an article called "Iran's President Launches Weblog." His statements were in Persian, Arabic, English, and French. He told of how he was born poor and became a good student. He criticized the United States and called it the "Great Satan USA." In a poll, he queried readers on their thoughts about U.S. and Israeli intentions in the Middle East.

According to Nasrin Alavi, author of *We Are Iran: The Persian Blogs*, Farsi is the fourth-most frequently used language for keeping on-line journals, or blogs. She wrote:

> Blogging in Iran has grown so fast because it meets the needs no longer met by the print media; it provides a safe space in which people may write freely on a wide variety of topics . . . some prominent writers use their blogs to bypass strict censorship and to publish their work on-line; established journalists can post uncensored reports on their blogs; expatriate Iranians worldwide use their blogs to communicate with those back home, and student groups and NGOs utilize their blogs as a means of coordinating their activities.[101]

In 2003, Iran became the first government to take direct action against bloggers, when they arrested and imprisoned a man named Sina Motallebi. When released, he moved with his family to Europe. After leaving, he learned that authorities had arrested his elderly father. Authorities are using their old tactics of arrests and intimidation. The head of the Iranian judiciary, Ayatollah Shahrudi, announced new laws pertaining to the Internet in October 2004. The law stated that "anyone propagating against the regime, acting against national security, disturbing the public mind and insulting religious sanctities through computer systems or telecommunications would be punished."[102]

That was not the case in 2003, though, when the bloggers in Iran spread the news of Shirin Ebadi winning the Nobel Peace Prize. Alavi said,

> Many young people view Ebadi as a daring heroine standing up to the ideological state. Within minutes of the announcement by the Nobel Prize Committee, bloggers were posting messages of congratulations. Items about Ebadi's prize dominated the Top Ten Rankings of an Iranian statistical analysis Web site, http://www.damasanj.com. It was the bloggers who passed the word to meet her incoming plane at the MehrAbab Airport in Tehran.[103]

On August 8, 2006, a brief article appeared in the *New York Times International* that said, "Rights Group Led by Nobel Peace Prize Laureate Banned." The Interior Minister of Iran said that the Defenders of Human Rights Center, which defends journalists and dissidents and criticizes hardliners, did not have a valid operating permit. "Its activities are illegal and the violators of this decision will be prosecuted."[104] Ebadi responded that the center did not need a permit under the constitution. Abdolfattah Soltani, a founder of the group, however, was sentenced to five years in prison in July for opposing the state and disclosing confidential information to diplomats.

Shirin Ebadi smiles while displaying the German translation of her memoir, titled *Iran Awakening: A Memoir of Revolution and Hope* in English, in this photograph from 2006. Ebadi continues to be active around the world in pursuit of her goal to improve human rights.

Shirin Ebadi knows the power of the Internet. On August 10, 2006, another headline on the Web read, "Shirin Ebadi, Iranian Nobel Peace Prize Winner, Says She's in Danger of Arrest." It was an article about the ban on the Defenders of Human Rights Center, which Ebadi co-founded in 2002. Her appeal that the world be aware had the potential to be seen by billions of people. "There is a high possibility that they will arrest us," she said.[105]

The news of the Iranian government's actions inspired an editorial in the *New York Times* on August 15, 2006, in which the author's opening line was, "Under cover of the international furor over its nuclear activities and its support for Hezbollah,

Legacy of the Peacemaker

Shirin Ebadi has single-handedly changed the lives of women and children in Iran. Through tireless efforts, she has persevered in her endeavors to change laws, or at least ease some of them, so that women can divorce when they need to, and children of divorce can remain with their mothers longer. She has, case by case, brought attention to political dissenters and other prisoners who are tortured and murdered in Iran's prisons. For women and children, and political activists, she has created organizations within the country to help them. She is a role model to millions of young Iranian women who are seeking to change their country to a democratic one through their protests and writings.

Her memoir, *Iran Awakening: A Memoir of Revolution and Hope,* published in the United States by Random House, is an eloquent account of a woman who rose from a middle-class background in a repressive society to fight the giants of the world. She wrote from the heart, making her story universal, and people all over the world have responded. Her most recent focus on world peace will have a lasting impact. She is the mouse standing between two mighty and territorial lions issuing bellicose remarks, calmly explaining to millions of people that war is foolish and fruitless.

Iran is trying to silence its most prominent human-rights activist, and, by extension, all of the Iranians who speak for fundamental rights."[106] Many have seen or heard Shirin Ebadi speak, have read her memoir, or have read articles about the work she is doing under the most dangerous of circumstances. They all shudder when they read of the latest attack on this woman, who stands under five feet tall, yet was referred to by a *New York Times* book critic as "a towering figure."[107]

Shirin Ebadi knows to glance behind her as she walks, even with 14 bodyguards following her everywhere she goes in Iran. She can joke that they protect her, but at the same time, she knows they report her every move to the Iranian government. The headline of a *New York Times* editorial was "Who's Afraid of Shirin Ebadi?" The universal prayer is that her government, if not afraid of her, is frightened enough of international public opinion not to kill her.

Nobel Prize Acceptance Speech:
Shirin Ebadi

In the name of the God of Creation and Wisdom:

Your Majesty, Your Royal Highnesses, Honourable Members of the Norwegian Nobel Committee, Excellencies, Ladies and Gentlemen,

I feel extremely honoured that today my voice is reaching the people of the world from this distinguished venue. This great honor has been bestowed upon me by the Norwegian Nobel Committee. I salute the spirit of Alfred Nobel and hail all true followers of his path.

This year, the Nobel Prize has been awarded to a woman from Iran, a Muslim country in the Middle East.

Undoubtedly, my selection will be an inspiration to the masses of women who are striving to realize their rights, not only in Iran but throughout the region—rights taken away from them through the passage of history. This selection will make women in Iran, and much further afield, believe in themselves. Women constitute half of the population of every country. To disregard women and bar them from active participation in political, social, economic and cultural life would in fact be tantamount to depriving the entire population of every society of half its capability. The patriarchal culture and the discrimination against women, particularly in the Islamic countries, cannot continue forever.

Honourable members of the Norwegian Nobel Committee!

As you are aware, the honor and blessing of this prize will have a positive and far-reaching impact on the humanitarian and genuine endeavors of the people of Iran and the region. The magnitude of this blessing will embrace every freedom-loving and peace-seeking individual, whether they are women or men.

Today coincides with the fifty-fifth anniversary of the adoption of the Universal Declaration of Human Rights; a declaration which begins with the recognition of the inherent dignity and the equal and inalienable rights of all members of the human family, as the guarantor of freedom, justice and peace. And it promises a world in which human beings shall enjoy freedom of expression and opinion, and be safeguarded and protected against fear and poverty.

Unfortunately, however, this year's report by the United Nations Development Programme (UNDP), as in the previous years, spells out the rise of a disaster which distances mankind from the idealistic world of the authors of the Universal Declaration of Human Rights. In 2002, almost 1.2 billion human beings lived in glaring poverty, earning less than one dollar a day. Over 50 countries were caught up in war or natural disasters. AIDS has so far claimed the lives of 22 million individuals, and turned 13 million children into orphans.

At the same time, in the past two years, some states have violated the universal principles and laws of human rights by using the events of 11 September and the war on international terrorism as a pretext. The United Nations General Assembly Resolution 57/219, of 18 December, 2002, the United Nations Security Council Resolution 1456, of 20 January, 2003, and the United Nations Commission on Human Rights Resolution 2003, 68, of 25 April 2003, set out and underline that all states must ensure that any measures taken to combat terrorism must comply with all their obligations under international law, in particular international human rights and basic freedoms, special bodies and extraordinary courts, which make fair adjudication difficult and at times impossible, have been justified and given legitimacy under the cloak of the war on terrorism.

The concerns of human rights' advocates increase when they observe that international human rights are breached not only by their recognized opponents under the pretext of cultural relativity, but that these principles are also violated in Western democracies, in other words countries which were themselves among the initial codifiers of the United Nations Charter an the Universal Declaration of Human Rights. It is in this framework that, for months, hundreds of individuals who were arrested in the course of military conflicts have been imprisoned in Guantanamo, without the benefit of the rights stipulated under the international Geneva conventions, the Universal Declaration of Human Rights and the [United Nations] International Covenant on Civil and Political Rights.

Moreover, a question which millions of citizens in the international civil society have been asking themselves for the past few years, particularly in recent months, and continue to ask, is this: Why is it that some decisions and resolutions of the UN Security Council are binding, while some other resolutions of the council have no binding force? Why is it that in the past 35 years, dozens of UN resolutions concerning the occupation of the Palestinian territories by the state of Israel have not been implemented promptly, yet, in the past 12 years, the state and people of Iraq, once on the recommendation of the Security Council, and the second time, in spite of UN Security Council opposition, were subjected to attack, military assault, economic sanctions, and ultimately, military occupation?

Ladies and Gentlemen,

Allow me to say a little about my country, region, culture and faith.

I am an Iranian. A descendant of Cyrus the Great. The very emperor who proclaimed at the pinnacle of power 2,500 years ago that ". . . he would not reign over the people if they did not wish it." And [he] promised not to force any person to change his religion and faith and guaranteed freedom for all." The Charter of Cyrus the Great is one of the most important documents that should be studied in the history of human rights.

I am a Muslim. In the Koran the Prophet of Islam has been cited as saying:

"Thou shalt believe in thine faith and I in my religion." That same divine book sees the mission of all prophets as that of inviting all human beings to uphold justice. Since the advent of Islam, too, Iran's civilization and culture has become imbued and infused with humanitarianism, respect for the life, belief and faith of others, propagation of tolerance and compromise and avoidance of violence, bloodshed and war. The luminaries of Iranian literature, in particular our Gnostic literature, from Hafiz, Mowlavi [better known in the West as Rumi] and Attar to Saadi, Sanaei, Naser Khosrow and Nezami, are emissaries of this humanitarian culture. Their message manifests itself in this poem by Saadi:

> The sons of Adam are limbs of one another
> Having been created of one essence.
> When the calamity of time afflicts one limb
> The other limbs cannot remain at rest.

The people of Iran have been battling against consecutive conflicts between tradition and modernity for over 100 years. By resorting to ancient traditions, some have tried and are trying to see the world through the eyes of their predecessors and to deal with the problems and difficulties of the existing world by virtue of the values of the ancients. But, many others, while respecting their historical and cultural past and their religion and faith, seek to go forth in step with the world developments and not lag behind the caravan of civilization, development and progress. The people of Iran, particularly in the recent years, have shown that they deem participation in public affairs to be their right, and that they want to be masters of their own destiny.

This conflict is observed not merely in Iran, but also in many Muslim states. Some Muslims, under the pretext that democracy and human rights are not compatible with Islamic teachings and the traditional structure of Islamic societies, have justified despotic governments, and continue to do so. In fact, it is not so easy to rule over a people who are aware of their rights, using traditional, patriarchal and paternalistic methods.

Islam is a religion whose first sermon to the Prophet begins with the word "Recite!" The Koran swears by the pen and what it writes. Such a sermon and message cannot be in conflict with awareness, knowledge, wisdom, freedom of opinion and expression, and cultural pluralism.

The discriminatory plight of women in Islamic states, too, whether in the sphere of civil law or in the realm of social, political and cultural justice, has its roots in the patriarchal and male-dominated culture prevailing in these societies, not in Islam. This culture does not tolerate freedom and democracy, just as it does not believe in the equal rights of men and women, and the liberation of women from male domination (fathers, husbands, brothers . . .), because it would threaten the historical and traditional position of the rulers and guardians of that culture.

One has to say to those who have mooted the idea of a clash of civilizations, or prescribed war and military intervention for this region, and resorted to social, cultural, economic and political sluggishness of the South in a bid to justify their actions and opinions, that if you consider international human rights laws, including the nations' right to determine their own destinies, to be universal, and if you believe in the priority and superiority of parliamentary democracy over other political systems, then you cannot think only of your own security and comfort, selfishly and contemptuously. A quest for new means and ideas to enable the countries of the South, too, to enjoy human right and democracy, while maintaining their political independence and territorial integrity of their respective countries, must be given top priority by the United Nations in respect of future developments and international relations.

The decision by the Nobel Peace Committee to award the 2003 prize to me, as the first Iranian and the first woman from a Muslim country, inspires me and millions of Iranians and nationals of Islamic states with the hope that our efforts, endeavours and struggles toward the realization of human rights and the establishment of democracy in our respective countries enjoy the support, backing and solidarity of international civil society. This prize belongs to the people of Iran. It belongs to the people of the Islamic states, and the people of the South for establishing human rights and democracy.

In the introduction of my speech, I spoke of human rights as a guarantor of freedom, justice and peace. If human rights fail to be manifested in codified laws or put into effect by states, then, as rendered in the preamble of the Universal Declaration of Human Rights, human beings will be left with no choice other than staging a "rebellion against tyranny and oppression." A human being divested of all dignity, a human being deprived of human rights, a human being gripped by starvation, a human being beaten by famine, war and illness, a humiliated human being and a plundered human being is not in any position or state to recover the rights he or she has lost.

If the twenty-first century wishes to free itself from the cycle of violence, acts of terror and war, and avoid repetition of the experience of the twentieth century—that most disaster-ridden century of humankind, there is not another way except by understanding and putting into practice every human right for all mankind, irrespective of race, gender, faith, nationality or social status.

In anticipation of that day.

With much gratitude

Source: "Shirin Ebadi: The Nobel Peace Prize 2003," Nobelprize.org. Available online. URL: http://nobelprize.org/nobel_prizes/peace/ laureates/2003/ebadi-lecture-e.html. © The Nobel Foundation, 2003.

CHRONOLOGY

1947   *June 21* Shirin Ebadi is born.

1964   Ayatollah Khomeini is expelled from Iran.

1965   Ebadi graduates from Reza Shah Kabir School,
Tehran; enters law school, University of Tehran.

1969   Ebadi graduates from law school.

1970   She becomes one of Iran's first female judges.

1971   She receives a doctorate with honors in private
law from Tehran University.

1975   Ebadi marries Javad Tavassolian.

1979   Revolution; Ayatollah Ruhollah Musavi Khomeini
becomes supreme leader; American Hostage
Crisis creates an international uproar.

1980   Reza Shah, former ruler of Iran, dies in Egypt;
Iran enters war with Iraq; baby girl, Negar, is born
to Shirin Ebadi and husband.

1981   American hostages are released.

1983   Ebadi's second daughter, Nargess, is born.

1988   Iranian civilian airplane is downed by United
States; war between Iran and Iraq ends; Ebadi's
brother-in-law, Fuad, is assassinated.

1989   Ayatollah Khomeini dies.

1994   Ebadi publishes book, *The Rights of the Child: A
Study of Legal Aspects of Children's Rights in Iran.*

1995   Ebadi cofounds the Association for Support of
Children's Rights; she serves as president until
2000.

1997   Seyyed Muhammad Khatami is elected president.

1998   Reign of Terror takes place in Tehran.

1999   University students riot.

2000   Ebadi publishes *History and Documentation of Human Rights;* she is put in prison.

2001   She cofounds the Center for the Defense of Human Rights and becomes its president; she receives Rafto Prize (Human Rights Prize in Norway).

2003   Ebadi is awarded Nobel Peace Prize; students riot.

2004   She receives the following prizes, awards, and degrees: International Democracy Award; Lawyer of the Year Award; Doctor of Laws, Brown University; Doctor of Laws, University of British Columbia; Honorary Doctorate, University of Maryland; Honorary Doctorate, University of Toronto; Honorary Doctorate, Simon Fraser University; and Honorary Doctorate, University of Akureyri.

2005   Ebadi receives the following awards and degrees: Honorary Doctorate, Australian Catholic University; Honorary Doctorate, Concordia University; Honorary Doctorate, The University of York; Honorary Doctorate, Université Jean Moulin in Lyon; UCI Citizen Peacebuilding Award; The Golden Plate Award by the Academy of Achievement; Jean Mayer Global Citizenship Award from Tufts' Institute for Global Leadership.

2006   Ebadi publishes her memoir, *Iran Awakening: A Memoir of Revolution and Hope*, in the United States.

NOTES

Chapter 1

1. Elaine Sciolino, *Persian Mirrors: The Elusive Face of Iran.* New York: Free Press, 2000, 2005, p. 239.
2. Shirin Ebadi, with Azadeh Moaveni, *Iran Awakening: A Memoir of Revolution and Hope.* New York: Random House, 2006, p. 136.
3. Ibid., p. 137.
4. Ibid., p. xvi.
5. Ibid., p. 204.
6. Ibid., p. 205.

Chapter 2

7. Ebadi, *Iran Awakening,* p. 10.
8. Ibid., p. 9.
9. Lyn Reese, "Historical Perspective in Islamic Dress." Available at http://www.womeninworld history.com/essays.html
10. Ebadi, *Iran Awakening,* p. 9.
11. Ibid.
12. William Cleveland, *A History of the Modern Middle East.* Boulder, Colo.: Westview Press, 2004, p. 302.
13. Shiva Balaghi, "A Brief History of 20th Century Iran—Colonialism and Constitutionalism: Iran at the Turn of the Century." Available at http://www.nyu.edu/ greyart/exhibits/iran/brief history/body_index.html.
14. Ebadi, *Iran Awakening,* p. 5.
15. Ali Akbar Mahdi, "Fending for Themselves." Iranian.com. Available at http://go.owu.edu/ ~aamahdi/.

16. John L. Esposito, *Islam: The Straight Path.* New York: Oxford University Press, 1988. pp. 169–170.
17. Ebadi, *Iran Awakening,* p. 10.
18. Balaghi, "A Brief History of 20th Century Iran."
19. Goldbarg Bashi, "The 'Boom' in Prose Writing by Iranian Women Authors in the 1990s Within the Context of the Situation of Women in Contemporary Iran." Department of Middle Eastern Studies, The University of Manchester, Spring 2000.
20. Ebadi, *Iran Awakening,* p. 18.
21. Balaghi, "A Brief History of 20th Century Iran."

Chapter 3

22. Betty Friedan, "Coming Out of the Veil," *Ladies Home Journal* (June, 1975): p. 98.
23. Ebadi, *Iran Awakening,* p. 21.
24. William O. Beeman, "Iran and the United States: Postmodern Culture Conflict in Action." *Anthropological Quarterly,* vol. 76, no. 4 (Fall 2003): pp. 671–691. Social Thought and Commentary, Project Muse. Available at http://muse.jhu.edu.
25. Sciolino, *Persian Mirrors,* p. 163.
26. Ebadi, *Iran Awakening,* p. 29.
27. Ibid., p. 31.
28. Mohammad Mehdi Khorrami, Ph.D., "The Islamic Revolution." PBS Online. Available at http://www.internews.org/ visavis/BTVPagesTXT/ Theislamicrevolution.html.

29. Sciolino, *Persian Mirrors,* p. 48.
30. Bernard Lewis, *From Babel to Dragomans: Interpreting the Middle East.* Oxford, U.K.: Oxford University Press, 2004. p. 222.
31. Ebadi, *Iran Awakening,* p. 33.
32. Ibid., p. 35.
33. Sciolino, *Persian Mirrors,* p. 53.
34. Ebadi, *Iran Awakening,* p. 35.
35. Sciolino, *Persian Mirrors,* p. 47.

Chapter 4

36. Ebadi, *Iran Awakening,* p. 37.
37. Lewis, *From Babel to Dragomans,* p. 302.
38. Ziba Mir-Hosseini, "Shirin Ebadi's Nobel Peace Prize Highlights Tension in Iran." *Middle East Report Online,* October 27, 2003. Available at http://www.merip.org/mero/mero102703.html.
39. Iftikhar Ahmad, "Shirin Ebadi: A Musim Woman Nobel Peace Laureate," *Social Education,* vol. 68, no 4 (May 1, 2004): p. 260.
40. Ebadi, *Iran Awakening,* p. 39.
41. Ibid., p. 51.
42. Photius Coutsoukis, "Iran Education." Available online. URL: http://www.photius.com.
43. Ebadi, *Iran Awakening,* p. 46.
44. Christopher de Bellaigue, *In the Rose Garden of the Martyrs: A Memoir of Iran.* New York: Harper Collins, 2004, p. 80.
45. Ebadi, *Iran Awakening,* p. 46.

Chapter 5

46. Sciolino, *Persian Mirrors,* p. 178.
47. Ebadi, *Iran Awakening,* p.63
48. Sciolino, *Persian Mirrors,* p. 173.
49. Ibid, p. 61.
50. "Shaking Hands With Saddam Hussein: The U.S. Tilts Toward Iraq, 1980–1984," edited by Joyce Battle. National Security Archive (George Washington University). Available at http://www.gwu.edu/~nsarchiv.
51. Ebadi, *Iran Awakening,* p. 51.
52. Lewis, *From Babel to Dragomans,* p. 223.
53. Hashemi Rafsanjani, "Women, Islam, & Equality." The National Council of Resistance of Iran Foreign Affairs Committee. Available at http://www.iran-e-azad.org/english/book_on_women/chapter2.html, p. 11.
54. Ebadi, *Iran Awakening,* p. 82.
55. Sciolino, *Persian Mirrors,* p. 179.
56. Ebadi, *Iran Awakening,* p. 86.
57. Ibid., p. 89.

Chapter 6

58. Paul Klebnikov, "Millionaire Mullahs." Forbes. July 21, 2003. Available at http://www.forbes.com/forbes/2003/0721/056.html.
59. Ebadi, *Iran Awakening,* p. 111.
60. UNHCR (United Nations High Commissioner for Refugees). Available at http://www.unhcr.org/cgi-bin/texis/vtx/home.
61. Rafsanjani, "Women, Islam, & Equality," p. 12.
62. Ibid., p. 13.

63. Ebadi, *Iran Awakening*, p. 99.
64. UNHCR, p. 4.
65. Ebadi, *Iran Awakening*, p. 159.
66. Rafsanjani, "Women, Islam, & Equality," p. 14.
67. Ebadi, *Iran Awakening*, p. 108.
68. Ibid., p. 122.
69. Debra Pickett, "Sunday Lunch With . . . Shirin Ebadi." *Chicago Sun-Times* (May 14, 2006). Available at http://www.chicagoredstreak.com/output/pickett/cst-ns-lunch14.html
70. Ibid.
71. Ebadi, *Iran Awakening*, p. 117.

Chapter 7

72. Sciolino, *Persian Mirrors*, p. 81
73. de Bellaigue, *In the Rose Garden of the Martyrs*, p. 231.
74. Ebadi, *Iran Awakening*, p. 143.
75. Sciolino, *Persian Mirrors: The Elusive Face of Iran*, p. 187.
76. de Bellaigue, *In The Rose Garden of the Martyrs*, p. 231.
77. Sciolino, *Persian Mirrors*, p. 241.
78. de Bellaigue, *In the Rose Garden of the Martyrs*, p. 233.
79. Sciolino, *Persian Mirrors*, p. 15.
80. Ebadi, *Iran Awakening*, p. 152.
81. Ibid., p. 154.
82. de Bellaigue, *In the Rose Garden of the Martyrs*, p. 246.
83. Ibid.
84. Ebadi, Shirin, *History and Documentation of Human Rights in Iran*. New York: Bibliotheca Persica, 2000, p. ix.
85. Ebadi, *Iran Awakening*, p. 160.

Chapter 8

86. Ibid., p. 163.
87. Ibid., p. 168.
88. Ibid., p. 184.
89. Ibid., p. 198.
90. Ibid., p. 203.
91. Ibid., p. 204.

Chapter 9

92. Michelle Goldberg, "Any Attack on Iran Will Be Good for the Government." Available at http://servicespiegel.de/cache/international. May 15, 2006.
93. Bradford Plummer, "The Persian Puzzle: An Interview With Kenneth Pollack." *Mother Jones*, January 24, 2005. Available at http://www.motherjones.com/news/qa/2005/01/kenneth_pollack.html.
94. Ebadi, *Iran Awakening*, p. 213.
95. Mahnaz Kousah, *Voices From Iran: The Changing Lives of Iranian Women*. New York: Syracuse University Press, 2002, p. 227.
96. Michael Lumsden, "Lipstick Jihad: An Interview With Azadeh Moaveni." *Mother Jones*, March 9, 2005. Available at http://www.motherjones.com/news/qa/2005/03/moaveni.html.
97. Laura Secor, "The Young Iranians." Interview with Matt Dellinger. *The New Yorker*, November 21, 2005. Available at http://www.newyorker.com/online/content/articles/051121on_onlineonly01.

98. Kurt Nimmo, "O'Reilly: Mass Murder Is the 'Sane Thing to Do.'" March 11, 2006. Available at http://wbeeman.blogspot.com/2006_03_11_wbeeman_archive.html.

99. Secor, "The Young Iranians."

100. Ibid.

101. Nasrin Alavi, *We Are Iran: The Persian Blogs.* New York: Soft Skull, 2005, p. 1.

102. Ibid., p. 3.

103. Ibid., p. 280.

104. "Iran. Rights Group Led by Nobel Peace Laureate Banned." *The New York Times* *International,* August 8, 2006, p. A6.

105. "Shirin Ebadi, Iranian Nobel Peace Prize Winner, Says She's in Danger of Arrest." August 10, 2006. Available at http://direland.typepad.com/direland/2006/08/shirin_ebadi_ir.html.

106. Editorial, "Who's Afraid of Shirin Ebadi?" *The New York Times* (August 15, 2006).

107. Laura Secor, reviewer, "A Dissenting Voice"—Iran Awakening, by Shirin Ebadi. *The New York Times* (July 16, 2006).

BIBLIOGRAPHY

Afkhami, Mahnaz. *Faith & Freedom: Women's Human Rights in the Muslim World.* New York: Syracuse University Press, 1995.

Alavi, Nasrin. *We Are Iran: The Persian Blogs.* Brooklyn, N.Y.: Soft Skull Press, 2005.

Armstrong, Karen. *Islam: A Short History.* New York: Modern Library, 2002.

Brooks, Geraldine. *Nine Parts of Desire: The Hidden World of Islamic Women.* New York: Anchor Books, 1995, 2000.

Cleveland, William. *A History of the Modern Middle East.* Boulder, Colo: Westview Press, 2004.

de Bellaigue, Christopher. *In the Rose Garden of the Martyrs: A Memoir of Iran.* New York: HarperCollins, 2004.

Ebadi, Shirin. *History and Documentation of Human Rights in Iran.* New York: Bibliotheca Persica Press, 1999.

Ebadi, Shirin. with Azadeh Moaveni, *Iran Awakening: Memoir of Revolution and Hope.* New York: Random House, 2006.

Esposito, John L. *Islam: The Straight Path.* New York: Oxford, U.K.: Oxford University Press, 1988.

Kousha, Mahnaz. *Voices From Iran: The Changing Lives of Iranian Women.* Syracuse University Press, 2002.

Lewis, Bernard. *From Babel to Dragomans: Interpreting the Middle East.* Oxford, U.K.: Oxford University Press, 2004.

Pollack, Kenneth M. *The Persian Puzzle: The Conflict Between Iran and America.* New York: Random House, 2004.

Rafsanjani, Hashemi. "Women, Islam & Equality." The National Council of Resistance of Iran Foreign Affairs Committee. Available at http://www.iran-e-azad.org/english/book_on_women/chapter2.html.

Sciolino, Elaine. *Persian Mirrors: The Elusive Face of Iran.* New York: Free Press, 2005.

"Women Winners of the Nobel Peace Prize." Women in World History.com. Available online. URL: http://www.womenin worldhistory.com/contemporary-03.html.

FURTHER READING

Books

Beeman, William O. *The "Great Satan" vs. the "Mad Mullahs": How the United States and Iran Demonize Each Other.* New York: Praeger, 2005.

Milani, Farzaneh. *Veils and Words: The Emerging Voices of Iranian Women Writers.* New York: Syracuse University Press, 1992.

Moaveni, Azadeh. *Lipstick Jihad: A Memoir of Growing Up Iranian in America and American in Iran.* New York: Public Affairs, 2005.

Wright, Robin. *The Last Great Revolution: Turmoil and Transformation in Iran.* New York: Knopf, 2000.

Web sites

"A Brief History of Women's Movements in Iran 1850–2000," Payvand.com
http://payvand.com/women/

Country Studies
http://countrystudies.us/

Iran Chamber Society
http://www.iranchamber.com

Iranian.com
http://www.iranian.com

Mother Jones
http://www.motherjones.com

United Nations University: Institute of Advanced Studies
http://www.ias.unu.edu/events

PICTURE CREDITS

page

cover

INDEX

JANET HUBBARD-BROWN is a writer, an editor, and a teacher, who lives in Fayston, Vermont. She has written 20 books for children and young adults. Most recently, she has written biographies of Hernando de Soto, Scott Joplin, the Labonte Brothers, and Geoffrey Chaucer for Chelsea House Publishers. Her next project is a book on the United States Constitution. She is indebted to Alison McGandy Hafiez for sharing her expert knowledge on the Middle East.